Symbol and the Symbolic

Symbol and the Symbolic

Ancient Egypt, Science and the Evolution of Consciousness

R. A. Schwaller de Lubicz

Translated by Robert & Deborah Lawlor

Inner Traditions International
Rochester, Vermont

Inner Traditions International
One Park Street
Rochester, Vermont 05767

First published in France as *Symbol et Symbolique* © 1949 by R. A. Schwaller de Lubicz
Translation copyright © 1978 by Autumn Press, Inc.
Illustration copyright © 1978 by Lucie Lamy

Library of Congress Cataloging-in-Publication Data

Schwaller de Lubicz, R. A.
　　Symbol and the symbolic.

　　Translation of: Du symbole et de la symbolique.
　　Includes bibliographical references.
　　1. Symbolism. 2. Egypt—Miscellanea. I. Title.
BF1623.S9S3813　1981　　110　　　81-13375
ISBN 0-89281-022-X　　　　AACR2

Printed and bound in the United States

10 9 8 7 6 5 4

Distributed to the book trade in the United States by American International Distribution Corporation (AIDC)

Distributed to the book trade in Canada by Publishers Group West (PGW), Montreal West, Quebec

Distributed to the book trade in the United Kingdom by Deep Books, London

Distributed to the book trade in Australia by Millennium Books, Newtown, N. S. W.

Table of Contents

Translator's Introduction

THERE IS ONE precaution that can be given here to the reader drawn to the work of R. A. Schwaller de Lubicz for the first time. Schwaller de Lubicz is using words and thought forms that are peculiar to our present rationalized mentality but with the intention of describing or, rather, evoking in us a mentality completely different from our own, one that belonged to the sages of ancient Egypt. And it is for this reason, more than any other, that difficulties can arise for us in the reading. Generally, these two complementary mental operations can be designated as *analytical* (our present habitual mode) and the more ancient *analogical* mode, but these words must be taken in a deeper sense than that generally ascribed to them at present. Schwaller de Lubicz's writings, then, act as a "synapse" between these two polarities of intelligence, and one finds that a clear, logical exposition—be it architectural, scientific or mythological—will suddenly lift and expand into an immense interconnected thought-field of an extra-rational quality, in which the multiple simultaneous meanings, while inwardly felt, may no longer be available to our rational mind. These unannounced fluctuations between our two primary modes of knowing is at first disconcerting, but, if one persists (sometimes without really grasping the idea), one can obtain glimpses of a new relationship between inner knowing and sensory-based external analysis.

Derived from his extensive study of Egyptian monuments and hieroglyphic writing, Schwaller de Lubicz's theme of two qualitatively different minds inhabiting the human psyche has found very convincing support in recent brain research. Experiments with brain-damaged individuals has revealed a distinct separation or lateralization of cortical functions giving rise to an area of scientific investigation popularly known as "right and left mindedness."

> The left hemisphere processes information sequentially, the right hemisphere simultaneously, accessing several inputs at once. The left hemisphere works in series; the right in parallel. The left hemisphere is something like a digital computer; the right like an analog computer.[1]

This localization in the right hemisphere of the highly intuitive aspects of thought together with the capacity for non-verbal pattern recognition, is consistent with the dominant quality of mind which, in Schwaller de Lubicz's view, could have produced the temple architecture and hieroglyphic writing of the ancient Egyptians. Through myth, image and geometric proportion, Schwaller de Lubicz believed, the Egyptians were able to encapsulate in their writing and architecture the basic pattern structures of the natural universe.[2]

Brain research reveals that musical ability seems also to be located in the right hemisphere, particularly the recognition and recall of tone, harmony and melody. These musical aptitudes involve auditory pattern recognition of a holistic and often simultaneous nature, very different from the analytical and verbal processes which are located exclusively in the left hemisphere. The separation of the visual and verbal from the sonar and intuitive has deep implications in defining the difference between esoteric and exoteric knowledge.

Robert Ornstein of the Langley Porter Neuropsychiatric

1. Carl Sagan, *The Dragons of Eden*, (New York, Random House) p. 169.

2. See R. A. Schwaller de Lubicz, *The Temple in Man* (Inner Traditions, 1981) and *Le Temple de l'Homme* (Paris, Dervy Livres, 1977).

Institute has suggested that during our recent evolution the intuitive, non-verbal sensitivity of the right hemisphere has been obscured by the surge of active development in the left, analytical hemisphere. He claims that this imbalance in intracortical representation and communication might be considered a rudimentary cause for the conflicts, disorders and discrepancies which presently pervade our intellectual and social life.

In this brief work, Schwaller de Lubicz examines symbolism or, rather, the symbolic method in general, not from the point of view of our contemporary use of symbols as conventional designations, abbreviations or as literary, metaphoric devices, but as the means for transmitting a precise suprarational knowledge and intuitive vision which, he contends, was a major aspect of ancient science.

The symbolic attitude of ancient knowledge cultivated the intellect to the extent of perceiving all of the phenomena of nature itself as a symbolic writing revealing the forces and laws governing the energetic and even spiritual aspects of our universe.

Modern science, particularly subatomic physics, has, as Schwaller de Lubicz points out, expanded its knowledge of matter to the point where Nature must be considered suprarational (as being beyond the limits of rational methods and formulae). These new discoveries and ideas, he emphasizes, demand a new and as yet unfound vocabulary, as well as a radically different approach to education and knowledge itself. This view places Schwaller de Lubicz at variance with some contemporary writers such as Fritjof Capra who, in *The Tao of Physics,* contends that we can with our present scientific methods move directly into a science with spiritual dimensions. Schwaller de Lubicz denies this possibility, emphasizing that the achievement of a sacred science requires a transformation of mind which would considerably alter our relationship to knowledge and its expression. It is here that an understanding of the hieroglyphic intelligence of the Ancients may assist contemporary thought in surpassing the intellectual impasse presently incurred by our rational perception and methodologies.

Let us try to clarify the differences in the *symbol-making processes* belonging to each of these two mentalities, for undoubtedly the underlying theme of the book is an attempt to lead us from *reading* in our ingrained, logical, sequential manner toward the immediacy and sense of identity available through the hieroglyphic image. It is through the rich and exacting array of ancient hieroglyphic writing that analogical thought is lifted from subjective, poetic or personal insight to a precise, communicable, universal knowledge-activity upon which a science of nature can be founded.

Let us amplify this comparison. With our present form of writing we use groups of arbitrarily formed abstract symbols (our alphabetical letters) which convey memorized sound and visual associations. We are trained to think and communicate through these alphabetical letters—placed in certain (again, memorized) groupings, or words—by reducing these abstract conventions into objective images in our minds. Simply stated, this means that when we read *cat,* we immediately register the formed image: .[3] This habitual reduction from a nonobjective mental abstraction to a delimited image can be seen as an initially centripetal action, which, subsequently, disperses perception and knowledge into a classification of disconnected facts. We use numbers in a similar way, moving from abstract symbols to quantitative evaluations. But hieroglyphic writing works in the opposite or centrifugal direction. The image, the form, is there concretely before us, and it can thus expand, evoking within the prepared viewer a whole complex of abstract, intuitive notions or states of being—qualities, associations and relationships which cannot be described or defined but only experienced. A centering sense of unification

3. Even our most abstract or philosophical words need to be linked to image-forming words in order to convey meaning.

later results from this inwardly expansive movement of mind. A method of viewing is required comparable to our hearing faculty: one must learn *to listen to the symbolic image,* allowing it to enter into and pervade one's consciousness, as would a musical tone which directly resonates with the inner being, unimpeded by the surface mentality. In this moment of inner identity between the intellect and the aspect of the tangible world evoked by the symbol, we have the opportunity to live this knowledge.[4] "By the hieratic symbolic method the aim is no longer to translate things into sensory terms, but to put ourselves into the state 'magically' identical with the symbol-object, so as to become heavy with the quality of weight, to become red with the quality of redness, to burn with the quality of fire."[5]

These two mental processes then reverse the sequence of centrifugal and centripetal movements. The analytical mode first reduces abstractions to a defined image, followed by a proliferation of disconnected facts. The analogical mode, on the other hand, first expands from the image into far-reaching associations, then inwardly unifies. Lao-Tzu, who also lived in a hieroglyphic epoch, expressed this interplay thus: "In order

4. Recent experiments with dolphins give us an example of what we might consider as a purely sonar writing. In *Dragons of Eden,* Carl Sagan reports that ". . . dolphins and whales, who sense their surrounding with a quite elaborate sonar echo location technique, also communicate with each other by a rich and elaborate set of clicks whose interpretation has so far eluded human attempts to understand it. One very clever recent suggestion, which is not being investigated, is that dolphin/dolphin communication involves a re-creation of the sonar reflection characteristics of the objects being described. In this view a dolphin does not "say" a single word for shark, but rather transmits a set of clicks corresponding to the audio reflection spectrum it would obtain on irradiating a shark with sound waves in the dolphin's sonar mode. The basic form of dolphin/dolphin communication in this view would be a sort of aural onomatopoeia, a drawing of audio frequency pictures—in this case, caricatures of a shark. We could well imagine the extension of such a language from concrete to abstract ideas, and by the use of a kind of audio rebus—both analagous to the development in Mesopotamia and Egypt of human written languages. It would also be possible, then, for dolphins to create extraordinary audio images out of their imaginations rather than their experience."

5. R.A. Schwaller de Lubicz, "The Intelligence of the Heart," lecture given in May, 1956 at the Congrès des Symbolistes in Paris. Translated by Nancy Pearson, published in *Parabola,* vol. 2, issue 3, 1977.

to expand, one must first contract; in order to contract, one must first expand."

The outwardly projecting analytical mind, which grasps for fixed and quantified objectifications with relationships dependent on equational logic, was also well known to the ancient thinkers, but there seems to have been an effort to restrict its use. In the *Treatise on Initiations* attributed to Hermes Trismegistus, we find a dialogue between Hermes and the initiate Asklepios who asks:

> *Asklepios:* Are, then, not all men similarly conscient, Trismegistus?
> *Hermes:* All, Asklepios, have not the true intelligence. They are deceived when they suffer themselves to be drawn after the image of things, without seeking for the true reason of them. It is thus that evil is produced in man; and that the first of all creatures lowers himself almost to the level of brutes.[6]

In one phrase this Hermetic text reveals this intelligence (which Western society has exaggerated and upon which it has become dependent) as the source of evil in the world—evil being understood here as disorder, disharmony and obscurity existing between humanity, nature and God.

Obviously, a special training is needed to practice the Symbolic Method; moreover, an intentional reorientation and reeducation of the mind is necessary for humanity to progress in the direction of the expanded consciousness required by our evolution. The need for this growth of consciousness is presently imposed upon us by the crisis and confusion existing in all spheres of life—moral, philosophic, environmental, scientific. The first step toward changing our intelligence is to

6. Hermes Mercurius Trismegistus, *The Virgin of the World*, translated by A. Kingsford and E. Maitland, 1885 (reprinted by Wizard's Bookshelf, Minneapolis, 1977) p. 52. The Hermetic doctrine, a fundamental source for both early Christian mysticism and medieval alchemy, also has important parallels with the Hebrew and Greek Kabbalah and the Vedic tradition of India.

specify exactly the dangers, limitations and troubling implications of our present methods; the second, to seek out and understand precisely techniques of thought practiced in previous epochs which display a richer integration of body, mind and spirit. Schwaller de Lubicz's penetration of the Egyptian symbolic method may be of assistance in this urgently needed transformation.

In conclusion, it may be helpful to give an example of a hieroglyphic reading, drawn from another work by Schwaller de Lubicz, in which he amplifies the essential concepts presented here.[7] It should be noted first that not all hieroglyphics were clear depictions of particular species of animals, plants, et cetera. Often a single image would be made up of a collection of parts drawn from various species (the head of a lion with the body of a woman, for example, or the body of a quail with the head and wings of a duck). In this way the image as a whole could depict subtle combinations and interchanges occurring in the energetic activity of the play of nature. But we shall content ourselves here with the simple image of the jackal and observe the way the image expands in multilevels and far-reaching associations.

In civilizations such as ancient Egypt, what we in our present presumptuousness call "primitive animal worship" was not a worship of the animal itself, but a consecration made to the vital function which any animal particularly incarnates. It was not, in reality, a worship; it was a meditation used to support and clarify an essential function of nature, that is to say, a *Neter*, a god. The Egyptians saw the jackal as incarnating certain characteristics, functions and processes of universal Nature. The jackal is an animal which tears the flesh of its prey into pieces, which it buries and does not eat until they rot. From this real, observed behavior, it becomes a symbol for both a metaphysical and physical process: *digestion*. Digestion is one of a number of universal processes which all

7. *Sacred Science, the King of Pharaonic Theocracy* (New York, Inner Traditions, 1982).

forms born into nature must undergo (others include growth, assimilation, coagulation, decomposition, transformation). Egyptian wisdom teaches us that no being or form can begin the processes leading to rebirth before its form or bodily envelope has disintegrated. The jackal-headed Neter, Anubis, is always pictured leading the soul of the deceased into the first stages of the lower realms of the *dwat,* or world of transformations. In mummification, the organs of the deceased were removed, dehydrated, and placed in urns. The urn holding the intestines had a jackal drawn on it. The intestine also serves the function of digesting food already broken down in the stomach. The jackal also transforms putrified flesh into life-giving nourishment. "What would be poisonous for almost all other creatures in him becomes an element of life through a transformation of elements which are bringing about this decomposition."[8]

The jackal is also the symbol of judgment: it is called "the Judge" because, in eating, it performs a precise, innate discrimination, separating out the elements capable of transformation and future evolution from the elements that are untransmutable within their present cycle.

Digestion is a destructive process: it is an analysis, a breakdown of material forms into their constituent elements. Our analytically directed minds are "jackal" in function. Not only do we analyze our society as it undergoes a decomposition, but our analyzing, separating mentality is the force that is destroying it. We are disintegrating not only the atoms of matter, but our social institutions, the very characteristics of our own psychological makeup and physical well-being, and other forms, such as religion and spiritual teachings from many cultures. But perhaps we are performing this seeming desecration in harmony with the laws of nature, whereby the death of the old gives life to the new. The jackal, however,

8. Isha Schwaller de Lubicz, *HerBak,* (New York, Inner Traditions, 1979)

knows innately that the destructive analysis must be arrested at just the right moment. He must dig up the morsels, or else these pieces of flesh—or these phases in the collective life of humanity—may pass into an indigestible, untransmuted state of disassociation or chaos; then the possibility of a cyclic rebirth in a continuity from death to new life could be lost. The Egyptian sage would tell us that we must worship· the jackal function in us and find out from it, through identification, the precise timing and laws applicable in the delicate process of the transmutation of our epoch.

Modern brain research suggests that the separation of intellectual functions is a result of our evolutionary background, and it offers possible symbolic reasons for the use of these curious animal images in ancient art, mythology and hieroglyphics. If we cast Schwaller de Lubicz's theory into modern physiological terms, we could say that this imagery is in reality an analogical language depicting levels of somatic information derived from evolutionary experiences which have been inscribed in the neurophysiology and morphology of our brain. This brings his study of ancient symbolism into a synchronicity with the recent work of brain researcher Paul D. MacLean. MacLean has proposed that the triune anatomical division of the brain into hindbrain, midbrain and cerebral cortex parallels distinct functions which developed during successive phases of our evolution: the hindbrain (stem, pons, medulla and cerebellum), which controls the automatic and autonomic reactions particularly involved with territorial mechanisms of survival and agression evolved during our reptillian phase. The midbrain or limbic system, which contains the cranial endocrinal glands that govern sexual development, sleep, dreams, passions, pleasure and pain, emotions, anxiety and the early mental function of visual retention, emerged during the early mammalian period. Last to develop was the cerebral cortex, which controls conscious brain activities, reason, willful action, analysis, logic, calculation and voluntary mobility. Each new brain structure grew as a peripheral envelope encasing the older brain component. Beneath the cerebral cortex the two earlier forms are still performing as they did in our most remote ancestors.

> "The human brain," MacLean holds, "amounts to three interconnected biological computers," each with its own special intelligence, its own subjectivity, its own sense of time and space, its own memory, motor, and other functions. Each brain corresponds to a separate major evolutionary step. The three brains are said to be distinguished neuro-anatomically and functionally, and contain strikingly different distributions of the neurochemicals dopamine and cholinesterase.[9]

With this new scientific input we can more easily grasp Schwaller de Lubicz's claim that anamistic symbols of animal, bird and reptilian-headed deities were means for evoking particular qualities and "awareness phases" in the continuum of the evolution of human consciousness. As Carl Sagan proposes[10] ". . . the hallmark of a successful, long-lived civilization may be the ability to achieve a lasting peace among the several brain components." And as Schwaller de Lubicz indicates, Egypt and other cultures grounded in the symbolic method, were indeed, through symbols, educating the neurological structure of the brain to maintain an active, conscious connection not only between the bilateral lobes of the cerebral cortex, but also with the impulses and subliminal information received from the ancient and deeper limbic and reptilian centers, so that these aspects of our nature could be

9. Carl Sagan, op. cit., p. 55.

10. Carl Sagan, op. cit., p. 234.

integrated into the activity of our reasoning mind.

Experimental evidence thus indicates that contained in our brain are functioning vestiges of our most distant corporeal minds. As Schwaller de Lubicz suggests, we should think of these vestiges not only as animal drives and gross, inconscient aspects of our consciousness, but also as a vast instinctual intelligence of the laws of nature, that our animal and reptilian experience has left in us. Instead of repressing and ignoring the wholeness of our evolution, should we not pursue ways to incorporate the vast symbolic content of these ancient brains into our present intelligence?

Thus the symbol is a material representation of immaterial qualities and functions. It is an objectification of things subjective in us and subliminal in nature, awakening us to a perception of the world which may make us aware of a knowledge contained in our soul.

There are many who have foreseen the great intellectual and spiritual advances toward which humanity is now impelled. But in the work of Schwaller de Lubicz we are given a *direction,* not towards an abandonment of the rational faculties in yogic ecstasies, but of an integration of it with a higher, innate intelligence. This direction consists of "techniques of thinking" such as the laws of "crossing" and "inversion," the application of the principles of the "Present Moment" and of the "simultaneity of opposites," as well as a spiritual perception of the mathematical sciences. All of these require a yet unformulated utilization of symbols which may synthesize the two complementary modes of our intelligence, and thus stimulate and eventually give expression to this impending growth of consciousness.

Robert Lawlor

Illustrator's Introduction

R. A. Schwaller de Lubicz's essay *Symbol and the Symbolic,* which appeared in Cairo in 1951, clearly rested on Pharaonic philosophy—as he emphasized in his foreword. For this reason authentic illustrations of Pharaonic tableaus have been included in this new edition, not simply for aesthetic reasons, but in order to enable the reader to become immersed in the reality represented in these figures, a reality as alive today as it was in ancient times.

The contemplation of a few of these renderings offers insight into both the Egyptian mystery, and, strangely enough, into some of the most recent discoveries of modern science.

The modern reader will be quite astonished to observe that the strange figurations of the royal underground tombs, which for centuries remained mysterious and inexplicable, find, to the extent that science has progressed, an explanation expressed in twentieth-century terms.

Even today, however, certain points, such as those exemplified in the following tableau, remain obscure.

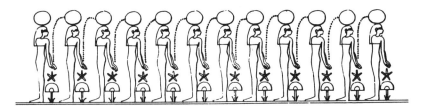

The Hours of RE are thus. Their forms are between their fingers (?),
their shadows are lower than their foreheads (?). They lead this

GREAT GOD in the West, whose forms are mysterious, toward their hours. They do what they have to do, [they] pass by and enter the earth, into the Cavern of He who hides his Hours, while their shadows carry their rays and their rays are in the flesh of him who hides them. The god has passed the bank. Those who follow [him], the souls, the guides of their bodies, enter into the darkness after the passage of Re .[1]

The inscription accompanying this strange figuration is indeed perplexing. We can readily sympathize with students of Egyptology who, after long years of study, have mastered the hieroglyphs and grammar—which make perfectly good sense when applied to "secular texts"—only to be faced with mythological texts at least as enigmatic as the representations they purport to explain.

Yet it is impossible to concede that the Ancients covered hundreds of meters of the walls and ceilings of the long corridors hollowed into rock, culminating at the tomb's Burial Chamber, with nonsensical figures. If we dismiss the view that these figures and texts are nonsense, we are then confronted with the possibility that we are dealing (as the texts themselves indicate) with a cosmogony summarizing the totality of the problems raised by the mystery of creation, a creation viewed as everpresent and constant. But as Alexandre Piankoff, one of the greatest specialists in the study of these texts observes, a great part of this cosmogony escapes us:

As in the missals of the Middle Ages, the Egyptians were often content to indicate by several words or a phrase a sacred text which the initiate or the priest had to recite by heart. But we are generally incapable of deciphering these symbols, which allude to Egyptian myths of which we have only a dim notion. The key to most of the great philosophic conceptions of the ancient world has been lost,. and we are often tempted to apply to these writings

1. A. Piankoff, *The Tomb of Ramses VI,* (New York: Pantheon, 1954) pl. 112–113, 116, and p. 332.

19

the vague term of mysticism. Now, we are not dealing with mysticism, but, as understood by the Egyptians of the New Kingdom, physics—physics which strangely recalls the ideas of Heraclitus of Ephesus. Indeed, as I compared the right and left walls of the Burial Chamber (of Ramses VI), this verse of Lucretius[2] came to mind: "the sun, after its passage under the earth, at the moment of its return to the horizon, casts forth its rays with which it strives to enflame the sky. Or, again, at the fixed hour, the fires are gathered together, concoursing regularly from numerous atoms of heat which each day produce a new sun, endowed with new light. Thus, it is said that from the high summits of Ida one perceives, at the birth of day, the scattered fires which then merge into a sort of singular globe and form a perfect disk."[3]

In a similar way, using certain keys which de Lubicz makes available, the modern viewer can begin to transcribe the strange imagery of the ancient figurations into the abstract formulas of the various laws and properties of matter and motion given to us by modern science. Thus, for example, we can interpret the predominant role ascribed in Egyptian mythology to negative and resistant entities such as Seth (the dark antagonist of Horus), the serpent Apophis, et cetera, as specific correlations with physical qualities, such as resistance, inertia, and entropy. Another specialist, intrigued with these negative entities, writes:

Why has revolt been conceived as an element of the creation, whereas it would have been simple enough to omit it, and thus assure a universe of eternal felicity? In fact, we find again here an idea that appears often in studying Egyptian texts: myth, at least in its most primitive form, is not a pure conception of the mind or spirit but often appears as a prescientific attempt to define and explain

2. Lucretius, *On Nature* 5.
3. A. Piankoff, *La Création du Disque solaire,* (Cairo: Institute Française d'Archéologie Orientale 1953) p. 1.

aspects of the universe and the forces that direct it. Now, disorder, storm, excessive or insufficient flooding [of the Nile], terrestrial or cosmic disasters are visibly part of the created universe.[4]

To summarize, those who have profoundly studied Pharaonic writings unanimously observe that the ancient Egyptians reveal, through their stories, figurations, and maxims, a form of thought that is balanced and clear when dealing with concrete life. Quite different, however, is Pharaonic theology, "from which logic is absent . . . ." But even if it accepts the nature of ancient myth as a "prescientific" attempt to explain the universe, the Western mind remains disconcerted by the lack of rational form in its presentation. The German Egyptologist E. Hornung offers a valuable insight in regard to this seeming inconsistency:

> According to western logic, it is an unthinkable contradiction for the believer to see the divine as the nearly absolute *Unique* and at the same time as the *Multiple;* it is surprising to us that the two forms of thought, so fundamentally different, do not annul each other, but appear, on the contrary, as complements . . . .[5]

Moreover, after having observed that every application of our dualistic logic to Pharaonic theology leads to insoluble contradictions, the same author arrives at the following conclusion:

> The notion of complementarity has long played an important role in the subject of an enlargement of classical logic. Neils Bohr introduced it into physics in 1927 in order to grasp the extravagant behavior of energetic quanta, and to explain the simultaneity of place, of impulsion, of wave and particle, which is impossible with the calculations of traditional logic.[6]

4. S. Sauneron, "Les Fêtes religieuses d'Esna," *Esna V* (Cairo, 1962) p. 266.
5. E. Hornung, *Der Ein und die Vielen* (Darmstadt, 1973), p.. 233-238 (as translated from the German by Lucie Lamy).
6. Ibid.

Paradoxically, the unmitigated empiricism of modern scientific method has reached an extreme at which its matrix formulas and methods, developed to explain a strictly materialistic worldview, are now providing a potent tool for resolving the metaphysical enigmas posed by ancient cosmogony.

Lucie Lamy

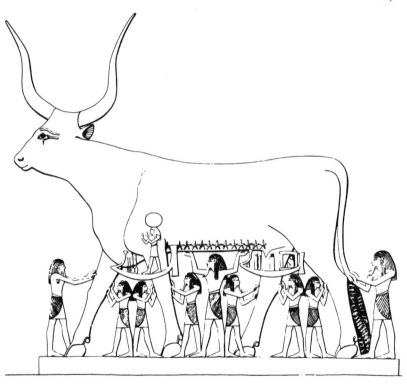

The Divine Cow, "the Beautiful", or Methyer, *"The Great Swimmer" in the celestial waves, mother of the Sun, whose morning and evening barques are seen at each end of the star-studded sky which she carries on her flanks. The sky is held up by* Shu, *the principle of Air and of Space.*

Preface

THE TRADITIONAL texts of initiation[1] can be read and studied in two ways. One of these deals with the exoteric (historic) meaning, which generally serves as a foundation, that is, as a symbol, for the esoteric sense (expressed through the symbolic) which these texts, legends, and representations would not have transmitted had the people seen them as nonsensical rather than as stories forming an image that they could understand and eventually disseminate.

Exotericism is thus a necessity, since thought needs support.

But when it is a question of penetrating the state of mind of an epoch or the *secret meaning* of texts (a meaning that is the basis of Egyptian knowledge, for example) only the symbolic can reach that far. The symbolic relies on artistic expression, on the themes of the representations, on architectural principles, on parables, legends, and other writings. The latter are presented in cabalistic form, one of whose aspects is addressed to the uninitiated, and can, for the most part, be transcribed.

As soon as the word *secret* is used, the question that comes up at once is, "What secret?"

Only twenty years ago it would be quite difficult to reply, since no one could understand that there might be advances in science without every discovery being placed at the disposition of the public. In fact, it is the "amateurs" who have long

1. For example, the Vedas and Gitas from India; Genesis, the Prophets, and other texts from the Hebraic Bible; the Gospels, the Apocalypse, and a good portion of the Epistles of the Apostles; the Pyramid Texts and many other Egyptian writings; representations in India, Babylon, Crete, Asia Minor, and especially Ancient Egypt.

contributed to the progress, not of science, properly speaking, but of its applications. Now, while a "mechanistic" science (and even the mechanics of molecules in chemistry) is within the grasp of every intelligence—pure science, the only science without ambiguity, once thought leaves the realm of a deterministic rationalism—is no longer accessible to everyone. In the past 30 or, at most, 40 years, the orientation of scientific thought has been completely modified, compared to what it still was in the last century.[2]

It is regrettable to see how few people are aware of the current revolution of thought, which will nonetheless influence the world to come—a revolution veiled by the large, immediate preoccupations (including the fear of atomic war) which affect all the realms of modern life.

The secret? But it is not contrived, it is evident. Who is capable of understanding the themes of the principle of relativity and their ramifications? Even among the great mathematicians, there are few capable of getting to the bottom of this study. Consider, then, the noble admission of Louis de Broglie,[3] when he says that, after studying Planck's constant for 25 years, he has not yet succeeded in "exhausting" the entire significance of the *quantum* of energy and action. The richness of certain "illuminations" of modern thought is such that it will be exhausted only with difficulty. This brutal evolution, which will place science in the hands of a very restricted elite, will create a new aristocracy in power after the proletarian endeavors and the emergence of a governing "technocratic" class, which are both, however, doomed to failure.

We see political power passing increasingly into the hands of very small groups of doctrinairians, and Russia is a valuable example of the logical outcome of the socialist principle, which becomes a proletarian dictatorship. But this is a question merely of a political power, opposite which there will

2. *Trans.*

3. Louis de Broglie, *La Physique nouvelle des quanta* (Paris: Flammarion, 1937) p. 5.

necessarily arise, curiously, scientific power. If the former can influence people's consciousness through force, the latter, far more tragic, will influence spiritual destiny, not through force, but through conviction. *Then the masses will no longer have any choice but to believe what only a small group of men will understand.* Believe and obey: this is already the case now, but obviously it will soon grow worse.

Is this not the "false temple," the false "religion," which is based, not on the Spirit, but on perishable matter and the science of its destruction?

Now no one wants this "religion," which nonetheless already exists and is spreading; ultimately, world government looks like the only general solution.[4] But already, for their part scientists no longer admit to being controlled by politics: it is they who hold the "secret."[5] This secret is not hidden from anyone, anymore than the esoteric teaching of Ancient Egypt was; one need only have developed the faculties needed to understand it. The example that present-day science offers us thus becomes an image for explaining the nature of the Temple of an esoteric science.

Let us not believe in the crocodile tears of scientists at the prospect of the destruction of humanity: these men know *that they can no longer stop in their research,* and that, having succeeded in the fission of heavy elements, they dream only of the fusion of light elements. They know that they must go all the way in freeing the Energy that "God" imprisoned in matter.

This consideration allows us to envisage two positions: that which believes in a constructive, liberating science, a science of *genesis;* and that which accepts a purely rational, analytical science, a science of violent *destruction.* Egypt, seen in this light, seems to have been the greatest center of the Masters of creative science. This explains its extreme importance at present,

4. Winston Churchill advocated the institution of a world super-government in the course of a speech delivered at Copenhagen on October 11, 1950.

5. Note, in this connection, various communications made to the press by Albert Einstein.

and we could not look to a more explicit or more perfect source.

Egypt has a special interest for the seeker since it still offers its ruins, intact texts and monuments. The texts of the pyramids of the Fifth Dynasty are carved very clearly in the stone; no hand has come along and changed the slightest mark. Thus, we are dealing here with documents unique in the world, the most ancient that have been handed down to us with this purity.

Now, over the past century, experience has shown that, despite the great number of documents brought to light and despite the efforts made to penetrate pharaonic thought, there is, in the translation of the texts, a great deal that makes no sense; complete mystery prevails as to the real meaning of the representations, the pantheon, and the myths, and, finally, as to the motive behind this colossal work of temples, steles, obelisks, and colossi extending for 2,000 kilometers along the Nile.

We stand before a strongbox containing the greatest wealth concerning the history of humanity; we have not been able to open it, because we have insisted on using the rationalist key, rather than that which the makers of this jewelcase used—the symbol and the symbolic.

It is true that the symbolism has given rise to many strange notions, warranted by the fact that its meaning is little known.[6]

6. Many attempts were made to penetrate the meaning of the pharaonic enigma by interpreting images and figures by means of symbolism. Here the door remained open to errors due to subjective judgements, because it is difficult, in this domain, to remain positive. It is evident that an effort was made to base each attempt on a guiding theory, which sometimes took on the character of a more or less coherent philosophy.

Later, rationalism thought that it could reject these attempts in their entirety, being convinced that, with Champollion's discovery of a logical reading, it would be easy to see clearly into the Egyptian mode of thought. It was therefore translated into our modern languages, in the modern spirit, and, moreover, it was thought possible to translate, solely on the basis of grammar, texts reserved for the temples. This has revealed nothing: neither the true mentality of the Ancients, nor their real knowledge of the forces of Nature. The same difficulties have been encountered here as in the translation of the Hindu texts of the Vedas and Upanishads, etc., or the text of Lao-

The symbol is a sign that one must learn to read, and the *symbolic* is a form of writing whose laws one must know; they have nothing in common with the grammatical construction of our languages.

It is a question here, not of what might be called "hieroglyphic language," but of the *symbolic,* which is not an ordinary form of writing.

The purpose of the next few pages is to describe briefly the principles that govern the symbol and the symbolic in the expression of a vital philosophy, not a rationalist philosophy. This will perhaps enable us one day to recognize that there exists no *hieroglyphic language,* but only a *hieroglyphic writing,* which uses the symbol to lead us toward the symbolic.

---

tzu's *Tao Te Ching* in China. All these writings are based on the intention of leaving up to the eventual reader the choice of interpretation, and of selecting, by this means, those morally and spiritually inclined to understand the true meaning. Often these texts are presented in a kind of "telegraph style," showing no grammatical connection between the substantives—that is, *avoiding the grammatical guide of thought.* Now, compared to the Hindu texts (which, moreover, have generally been transcribed several times), Ancient Egypt offers the advantage of the symbolic method of the form of writing. Without even concerning himself with an alphabetical system, the seeker can be guided by the symbol alone, provided that he take into account the essential principles that this book attempts to formulate. It is certainly a grave error to imagine that one can reject the symbolic because one believes that one has knowledge of a form of writing that expresses thought as do our alphabetic languages, which overlook the esoteric transcription of the image-filled symbolism.

Notes on Modern Thought

FOR THE FIRST time (exoteric) scientific research has reached, through rationalism, the threshold of a door which allows us to glimpse the intimate life of matter. Thus, it is indispensable for us to become acquainted with the present-day science, even if only by means of a general overview. It would, however, be a mistake to let oneself be permanently led astray by a science which cannot cross the border defined by the obligation always to rely on a system of references. But we must recognize that a great step has recently been made in the "expansion" of human consciousness; in fact, it is a question not only of an enormous scientific advance, but above all of an extremely important stage in the evolution of consciousness. It is not the acquisition of a knowledge base of an invariable nature; it is a new starting point for the progress of thought.

The present stage of this progress, the cause of the serious revolution undergone by scientific thought for about three decades, allows us to distinguish the principles that underlie the real meaning of the symbol. What, only yesterday, could be taken as pure philosophic speculation is today based on scientific experiment, with staggering consequences that few people are as yet aware of, since most remain faithful to the rationalist determinism of the 19th century.

The last century was characterized by the skyrocketing importance of science, which thinks itself capable of explaining all the phenomena of Nature, based on the "mechanistic" thinking that it is possible to predict the course of a phenomenon when the conditions of its manifestation are known. This "determinism" justified all hopes, even that of succeeding in knowing the development of the living cell and ultimately the secret of life. This science was founded on laws deduced from the behavior of matter, acknowledging that this matter was composed of atomic particles forming specific, invariable chemical elements, whose essential reactions were believed to be known, thanks to all the great chemists of the past century who relied on Lavoisier's famous statement, "Nothing is created, nothing is destroyed."

Thermodynamics and electricity, studied earnestly, were at the service of the science of a three-dimensional (Euclidean) matter, and what had been learned allowed one to hope that the remaining unknowns, as well as the exceptions in the experimentation of accepted hypotheses, would one day be cleared up. The only acceptable guide for the scientific mind, having become purely experimental, was a logical conclusion derived from experiment. All philosophy and research concerning the "why," necessarily leading to the metaphysical stage, was ultimately considered as fanciful extrapolation.

The "secret" and the "sacred" seemed like nonsense, and anti-religious tendencies developed, since human science could do everything, or at least it hoped someday to acquire this omnipotence. Under the cover of atheism, man substituted himself for God, since his Cause and his End were none other than his present existence.

If one wishes to understand the new state of mind, it is important to observe the mentality of this mechanistic science. This point was reached toward the end of the century, when Becquerel, by observing the discharge of an electroscope at the approach of a uranium salt, deduced radioactivity. Roentgen discovered that matter is transparent to cathode rays, which he called x-rays, the unknown. Curie, starting with uranium oxide, isolated an extremely radioactive salt, which he called the metal "radium." Then came Sir Oliver Lodge, Sir J. J. Thomson, along with Lord Rutherford, et al. in England, Perrin in France, Bohr in Denmark, Planck in Germany, Einstein in Switzerland (to cite only those names which are universally known)—the initiators of the science of microphysics (the study of the energetic atom) when the old simplistic conception of the material atom disappeared.

This is the dawn of a new era. Experiments will show that the physical laws of macroscopic matter are not universal, that the phenomenon can no longer absolutely be placed within the framework of a deterministic physics, and, finally, that there is a metaphysical element, Energy, which comes into play in the development and disappearance of matter.

Prominent men, physicists and philosophers, have now published in an assimilable form the information that emerged from the recently gained knowledge concerning this science,[1] so that ignorance of these new elements becomes a lacuna prejudicial to the conclusions of all research, even in archaeology.

Experimental science now has to deal with a new world of an abstract nature, a world whose elements can no longer be defined except mathematically.

It has been observed that electronic quantities disappear in order to make photons (light) of pure quantity-less energy, appear. Thought should intervene to find out what is implied in the phenomenon observed; today philosophy should guide experimentation. In physics, it is a question of a mathematical philosophy, but the impossibility of coordinating abstract elements, for which one has no definite concept,

1. "Microphysics" signifies the physical science of the atom, thus becoming nuclear physics. In this atom can be recognized, in principle, a nucleus comprising a neutral mass (neutron) and the positive electron (positron) maintaining in equilibrium a series composed of no more than seven layers of negative (electric) electrons.

Yet one should not take this information literally and believe that the current notions about the atom are definitively proved and certain. All that is known is that henceforth one must reckon with laws other than those determined in the material world. And since it is a question of the atom of the "constituent of matter," there is then—beyond what our senses observe—a state of a polydimensional nature that escapes us, which the cerebral (objective) intelligence can no longer grasp, but whose existence is indisputably certain and can be transcribed only mathematically. Does this not represent a radical upheaval of the conceptions of only 30 years ago?

requires that philosophy be used to seek the connection, the Ariadne's thread indispensable in this labyrinth of the world of energy recently revealed. Men like Lecomte du Noûy, Le Roy, and Gaston Bachelard, among others, are providing impetus for the new thought. Strange glimmers reappear, emerging from the medieval darkness of the time when the Masters of "Natural Philosophy" taught on the fringes of scholasticism.

Thus it can be observed that there are at most seven electronic layers around the atomic proton, recalling the sevenfold planetary system and its metallic correspondences, the musical scale, colors, etc. Let us add to this the seven fundamental constants: e, charge of the electron; m, mass of the electron; M, mass of the proton; h, Planck's constant; c, speed of light; g, constant of gravitation; λ, cosmic constant.

Now, it is the "constant" of which Henri Poincaré had a presentiment and which was determined by Professor Max Planck, that plays a leading role, especially in the discoveries of Louis de Broglie. Planck's constant (h) is, in brief, an invariable ratio between the Energy (E) of a photon and the duration (d) of its vibration, such that $E \times d = h$, whatever the wave or the color of the light is, or the wave of any other radiation.[2] By designating the inverse of the duration, that is, the frequency, from ν we get $E = h\nu$, and $h\nu$ is the quantum of Energy, that is, the smallest quantity of Energy whose multiples constitute the whole. If E diminishes, d increases, and vice versa. This "quantity" of Energy is the current basis for all reasoning in microphysics. This theory of the Quanta of Energy, broadened into the principle of the *quantum of action,* later worked on by Einstein and Bohr, is one of the finest "illuminations" of the scientific spirit of the times. Then, founded on these bases, it is certainly the discovery of Louis de Broglie,[3] along with that of Heisenberg, that most disturbs

2. These waves have lengths ranging from 50 kilometers to 1/100,000,000 millimeter. Beyond this are the γ rays.

3. Cf. Louis de Broglie, *Lumière et matière; La physique nouvelle des quanta,* (Paris: Flammarion, 1925).

the complacency of the "mechanistic" scientists, since the study of light shows the *simultaneous existence of two contradictory states:* the *granular* character in the *continuity* of a wave; that is, the photon, that looks like an isolated quantity, appearing in a continuous function of the wave—the discontinuous within the continuous. It is this simultaneity—that "cerebral" intelligence cannot grasp, but the existence of which is shown by experiment—that brings about what the physicist Werner Heisenberg calls the "Uncertainty Principle," which I shall translate here, psychologically, as the "Present Moment."

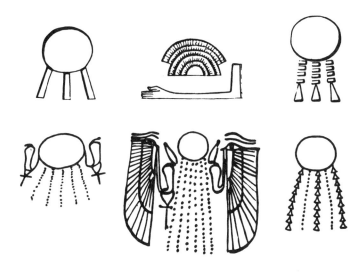

Fig. 1. Upper row, from left to right: hieroglyph determining the word sty, *"to beam", "to radiate, to shine"; hieroglyph used to write* khâ, *"to appear" (This sign represents a luminous source emitting spherical waves expanding into the air. Cf. the undulatory properties of light (interference, diffraction) described by Huyghens and Fresnel.); determinative hieroglyph of all the words designating light (cf. the corpuscular properties of light as described by Lucretius, Newton, Einstein). Lower row: paintings designating the sun.*

Heisenberg's uncertainty principle can be explained thus: if it is possible to locate precisely a moving object at a given moment, it is no longer possible to know its exact speed at this moment. Inversely, if one can specify the speed of a moving object at a given moment, then it will be impossible to know its exact location.

Certainly it is a matter of intra-atomic phenomena. The fact of observing the location of the electron—or at least the probability of its position—signifies an action in regard to it, which modifies it or changes its course. Thus, the fact of observing the phenomenon modifies its nature, so that, at a given moment, only one of the two elements can be known exactly: either its location or its speed. We can later "group" these data, separately observed, in order to acknowledge the simultaneous phenomenon without really knowing it.

Today this uncertainty principle plays a leading role in scientific thought. The faith that we placed in mechanistic determinism in the last century has given way to a doubt that opens the door to philosophy.

Heisenberg also plays a truly "iconoclastic" role in microphysics. He rejects all *imagination,* and hence the assumption that electrons possibly move circumferentially, in the manner of planets, around a nucleus or sun (as Bohr acknowledged) when it is known for certain only that there are "layers" with varying potentials.

The "uncertainty principle," does not enable us to locate the electron when it is moving at full speed; thus, we can know its location only as a probability. Heisenberg excludes the aspect that is in fact unknowable and is satisfied with the knowable aspect of the differences in energy potentials. In defining the atom—or, more exactly, its nature—thus, solely by the numbers representing these energetic values of the various electronic "layers" or stages, he counters a concrete, *assumed* image with a purely mathematical "matrix image" corresponding to the observable fact.

But let us continue this brief enumeration of a few principles, basic points of the new thought, in order to render the conclusion that can be drawn from it more comprehensible. Our old laws no longer apply to the atom—that is, the constituent of matter. They remain valid for matter, but in the atom, for example, Newtonian gravitation no longer plays a part: it is the electromagnetic effects that come into play. This is a fact, but one that needs to be studied, for we are still confronted with the unknown that the "affinities" represent. On the other hand, the chemistry of Lavoisier is happily dead, since we now know that matter is constantly vanishing into energy and that energy ceaselessly creates matter (through transmutation into isotopes). We know that in the upper atmosphere nitrogen is transmuted into an isotope of carbon, which then "nourishes" all vegetation—a fact that throws (or will throw) a curious light on to the "vital" phenomena on the earth's surface.

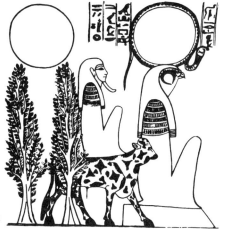

Fig. 2. "I know these two sycamores of turquoise between which Re comes forth, which grow on the swellings of Shu (the atmosphere) at this gate of the Master of the East." (Book of the Dead, Chap. 109). "Homage to thee, Sycamore . . . who captures what is in the Nw (the celestial ocean)." (Pyramid Texts, 1846). This group recalls "the nitrogen cycle," well known in agriculture.

Today we know something that people in the nineteenth century thought was no longer to be dreaded: we know that all our knowledge must be revised. It is quite certain that a new world has been revealed to the human spirit: but above all, it must be noted that new faculties of the intelligence are developing, and it is by this means that science can now penetrate further into the mystery of Nature.

We are no longer afraid to observe that a simple ray of light, reflected by a surface, is itself modified by modifying something in the atomic nature of this reflecting plane.

The new Chemistry, to which Physics has increasing relevance, is trying to find its way and, through hypotheses which are often quite strange, attempt to explain the combinations of atoms. We observe the same upheaval in Biology: Darwin's evolutionism cannot be corroborated; Lamarck's transformism, later enlarged upon by Haekel, is not proven; the doctrine of "genes" runs up against mutations.

In truth, everywhere, in an impassioned burst, people are "seeking," while *transposing the data onto a subtler level* than that of the arrogant, materialistic era of the previous century.

People are seeking everywhere *except in the teaching of the past,* where, in my opinion, is found the key, or at least the indication that can lead us towards the key of traditionalism, in order to guide the new thought.

Since this study has the symbol and the symbolic as its theme, one might be surprised to find questions concerning physics summarized here, questions with which philologists, who at present form the principle practitioners of Egyptology, usually do not concern themselves. But this superficial exposition of the present situation of the research in a pure science should make it clear that we are dealing not merely with a question of a new position of the seeker vis-à-vis experiment, but, above all, with a new state of thought, a new opening up of intelligence, which can be interpreted more or less in the following manner: the simultaneity of opposite states (complements) constitutes the phenomenon. Up until now, because of our objective position before this phenomenon, we have viewed it by splitting these two component states, in what I call "cerebral dualization," and it is on this "exotericism" that we built our purely analytical science; we would then call *synthesis* the "patching together" of elements isolated by analysis.[4]

Fig. 3. Seth, Master of the South, and Horus, Master of the North, the perpetual antagonists. Both of their heads emerge from a single body that stands on two horizontal bows evoking the energy potential that can make manifest the two inverse forces through the stimulation of the passage of Re.

With the "uncertainty principle" in observation and especially in the conclusions that we can actually derive from observation, and with the principle of the "discontinuous within the continuous" shown by light, the experimenter and later the philosopher must necessarily conclude that the "vital moment" of the phenomenon is characterized by the *contradiction* of its components. It thus becomes impossible to know the phenomenon in its genesis, if we do not call upon, within ourselves, a new form of intelligence which rejects objectification in order to replace it with abstract symbols. Now, this procedure obligatorily arouses in us the search for a "sensation" or a sort of "intuitive vision." Thus, the fact of being

4. Since "simultaneity" cannot be objectified, it cannot be "reasoned." Thus, even in Einsteinian relativity, the principle of scission remains.

obliged to accept this state of affairs in the study of nature already shows that human thought is progressing toward this new form of intelligence. In reality, esotericism is as old as humanity, but hitherto the state of intelligence of this esotericism belonged only to isolated individuals.

The impulsion toward the expansion of consciousness that our era is undergoing is probably the real, underlying reason for the disorder that reigns over the whole of our earth. Progress most certainly exists among those who deeply experience this state of incoherence, and it does not appear among those, who because of an instinctive, psychological reaction, cling to a dialectic materialism, a nihilistic mechanism. Collectivism, in the statistical sense, can no more solve social problems than it can scientific problems. The future demands an *individualism within the collective,* which seems absurd to the intelligence of the past. As for the expression, encyclopedic notes and museums of corpses are no longer satisfactory; what is needed is the *Symbolic,* which alone can effect a liaison between complements in the vital phenomenon.

And it is rational science, which today has reached what is already being called the surrational, that will open the way toward esotericism of a suprarational nature.

And if I consider that the *way* of pure science, in the current anxious research, is erroneous, I am, on the other hand, certain that the method of work is good with regard to the extreme precision and absolute fidelity of our scientists in their experiments.

After this brief and superficial enumeration of a few elements of the new thought, one might ask "What is the influence of this state of affairs on Egyptology, archaeology, and symbolism?"

Before I reply, here is what must be taken into account.

After the rather insolent certainty of the scientists of the nineteenth century, today's microphysicists are relatively timid. They are also the first to distinguish the new scientific thought from applied science in macrophysics, that science of matter for which yesterday's laws continue to suffice in practical and industrial application. This timidity on the part of our scholars in pure science is inspired by a respect for specialists. The philosophers of this new thought see further, and these philosophers are not fantasts.

It is certain that such a revolution in thought—that is, such an expansion of consciousness, such an evolution of intelligence—is not the result of a whim. It is in fact a question of a cosmic influence to which the earth, along with everything in it, is subjected. A phase in the gestation of the planetary particle of our solar system is completed. Gaston Bachelard observes, in this connection, what he calls "a mutation of the Spirit."[5] A new period must begin, and this is heralded by seismic movement, climatic changes, and finally, above all, by the spirit that animates man.

"Ogotemmêli" reveals to Marcel Griaule[6] the metaphysical basis of the customs of the Dogons, because he knows "that the time has come when these things, kept secret until now, must be said"; the Bambaras "speak";[7] the emperor of the Empire of the Serpents "speaks" to F. G. Carnochan.[8] But without visiting black Africa, which still holds many surprises for us, let us observe what occurs in our vicinity. No one is less concerned with mathematics and rational science than are artists, whether they be poets, musicians, painters, or sculptors. However, all the arts are in step with scientific thought; they all attempt to flee from a specific, realistic mode of expression; they all seek to appeal to the "intuitive sensa-

5. Gaston Bachelard, *Le Nouvel esprit scientifique* (Paris: Presses Universitaires de France), p. 178

6. Marcel Griaule, *Dieu d'eau, entretiens avec Ogotemmeli*, (Paris: Edition du Chêne, 1948.)

7. Solange de Ganay, "Notes sur la Théodicée Bambara," *Revue de l'histoire des religions*, vol. 135, nos. 2–3; "Aspects de mythologie et de symbolique Bambara," *Journal de psychologie normale et pathologique*, April–June 1949, pp.181–201.

8. F.G. Carnochan and H.C. Adamson, *L'Empire des Serpents* (Paris: Stock).

tion," by means of forms which are as simplified as possible, to the point of geometrical reduction.

Whoever thinks and "experiences" with any sensitivity will respond to this mysterious call of our time: the Idea dominates the form; *Spirit-Energy* dominates matter.

Accordingly, I would say to my Egyptologist and archeologist, historian or symbolist friends:

1. It has been demonstrated that without a philosophical directive no progress can be made in scientific investigation, whatever its nature. If this scientific philosophy is still "a posteriori," today there is nothing to prevent the fact—and mathematical thought allows it to be foreseen—that one day it may be experimentation that becomes "a posteriori," obeying the directive of a thought *that has solved the problems.*

This suggests an hypothesis: the application of science would once again become, as in Egypt and Hellas, an empirical science (that is, one without research into causes), *Knowledge being reserved for the Temple,* that is, for the select group of gifted men taught to penetrate this Knowledge because this penetration requires—as does our new scientific thought— *knowing first of all how to think without objectifying.* This is a stage in awaiting the expansion of Consciousness that will give spatial *vision.* In fact, it is obvious, for example, that the "matrix image" is merely a method and not a final attainment and that it should be possible "to objectify," *in a higher form of intelligence,* a continuum of four-dimensional volume just as well as we now do with Euclidean volume.

If evolution exists, it can only be an "evolution of Consciousness," and it is probably there that one should look for the cornerstone of the new biology, which we shall discuss some other time.

2. The observation of a simultaneity of mutually contradictory states, which we can only know through duality (that is, by means of comparison), demonstrates the existence of two forms of intelligence.

I propose the following explanation:

The first of these forms requires the object or the objectification of the concept, hence the placing of the concept in Time and Space. This form may be called "static intelligence," which is also designated as "exotericism."

The other form of intelligence conceives intuitively, but without yet *formulating* the concept. I call this form "innate knowledge"; it corresponds moreover to a certain way of seeing possessed by ancient Greek philosophers, particularly Heron of Alexandria.[9] They acknowledged that inscribed in the soul was the universal knowledge that the exterior object awakens through the senses. Now, it is precisely *the consciousness of the state of this innate knowledge which can vary,* that is, progressively expand and grow richer or poorer.[10]

As soon as the intuitive concept—which manifests as a certainty as concrete as an object can be—becomes formulated (that is, described and defined) it becomes static, "exoteric." Thus, the intuitive form of intelligence can be called "a dynamic intelligence," since it can conceive movement, such as a spherical spiral, which is objectively incomprehensible. In mathematics, these concepts are customarily called "imaginary," like, for example, the Axis, which is (we do well to note) unimaginable. This is, then, that "dynamic" intelligence which is called "esoteric."[11]

9. Heron of Alexandria, Definitions, 136, 1–4.

10. This is noted here without going into an analysis *showing what can sustain* this acquired consciousness.

11. Esotericism is outside the rational, and not surrational; it is on this side of and beyond the rational. It consists in a *consciousness, innate by virture of human genesis, throughout all the types of natural life.* For example, affinity is an innate knowledge. It is one of the original impulsions for the faculty of counting, which is an "a priori," but merely "exoteric," aspect of intelligence.

The faculty of reasoning has its source in the impulsion beyond the rational: esotericism is the cause of Consciousness in general. We carry within ourselves—in the form of acquired, latent knowledge—the experience of all the beings which, human embryology shows, successively presided over the formation of the human being.

There is an esotericism of Science, signifying the abstract sources of what can be known, and a science of Esotericism, which is the philosophy of causes.

These are realities to which the new scientific thought must conform. Thus, it becomes altogether logical to create a mathematical philosophy which excludes any objective formulation: the value expressed in a formula—whether an imperative or an equation—replaces any imagined or even unimaginable form. Moreover, the conventional symbol replaces long sequences of reasoning.

We have reached this point inevitably.

Also, inevitably, writing, which links the two states or forms of intelligence, is symbolic, since the *figured symbol*—all the more correct for being selected from natural forms—alone makes possible the link between exotericism and esotericism, a link that comes into play in every act of comprehension.

3. This profound epistemological[12] crisis—which we are experiencing and which can be interpreted parallel to the general revolution, which is moral as well as social and aesthetic—recalls another profound revolution at the end of the Egyptian era and the beginning of the Christian era.[13] What we are able to find out about the history of Ancient Egypt shows us a similar revolution on the eve of the Middle Kingdom,[14] circa 2200–2100 B.C. These three dates (the Egyptian date, the beginning of the Christian era, and our own time) correspond only too well in the revolutionary aspect

---

12. *Epistemology:* This term of philosophic language signifies what could be called "the mentality of the evolutionary stages of intelligence" which all of us carry within ourselves, through heredity. These stages, or "mentalities," change with the evolution of the intelligence. Thus, we carry in us a set of "mentalities" which guide us in our intellectual efforts. By noting the percentage of these influences, one could thus render an "epistemological profile or portrait" of each person. For example, a simple man will be influenced 70% by what is called the "mystical mentality," 40% by the "realistic sense," 20% by the "positive sense," 5% by the "rational sense," and 0% by the "surrational sense."

In this way one can know how this man will tackle the study of a problem.

N.B.: Here the word mystical means the tendency to attribute to "divine," occult powers—hence to the arbitrariness of these forces—all the phenomena of nature.

13. A similar crisis occurred at this time in China, with the end of the Han Dynasty, which was also a Bronze Age.

14. In this connection it can be interesting to read Junker, *Pyramidenzeit.*

of the *vital nature,* to the precessional cycles[15]—Taurus
(Montu), Aries (Amun), the end of Pisces (the Christian era),
today (in about 150 years)—for this correspondence between
the celestial dates and great events on Earth to be pure coincidence.

Now, if this is true, here is where the symbolic again
assumes an extraordinary value, as much in the figuration by
the signs of the zodiac as in Antiquity's choice of its symbolic
for the moment.

These crises are always profound, and they affect the whole
of humanity. It is not a question of a local revolution, such as
the French Revolution of 1789, which, despite its general
repercussion throughout the world, was only a precursory
event to what is happening today. Moreover, we note that the
great event of the precessional passage from one sign into
another is always preceded by preparatory events. The "fever"
starts in the last decanate, or 720 years before the "eruption."
Now, what is troubling today is that the current revolution
does not promise to be constructive. For example, the Christian era, based on a revelation, coming as a logical conclusion
after the Egyptian era, in fact stems from a revelation:[16] the
consciousness is enriched *before the application,* in all the
domains of human activity.

In our time, the application precedes the state of consciousness, which does not correspond to the material attainments;
there is disagreement between the dynamic and the static,
between the psychic and the cerebral, between esoteric and
exoteric intelligence. The crisis is extremely dangerous and
could be called that of an end of a world, containing an *annun-
ciation,* whereas the final crisis of the Egyptian Old Kingdom

---

15. Each cycle lasts approximately 2,160 years.

16. It is no longer a question of the evangelical revelation of the Divine, but of its
anthropo-morphization. This is characteristic of the end of the last decanate of the
Egyptian era (when in Greece and then in Rome the principal deities are humanized,
and divinized Man now *crowns* the temple, steles, and columns).

and that of the era of the Apostles were each the beginning of a new era.

This suggestion of a coincidence between the dates of the great celestial cycles and the events to which men on Earth respond would be difficult to accept if one were not aware of what is currently going on in the depths of human consciousness. The act of noting this in itself presents an extremely interesting foundation, even for historical study, and one necessarily consonant with the symbolic.

Before speaking of the symbol and of the principles that one must know in order to understand its psychology, it would be good to note first what meaning I give to the symbolic. "Symbolism," which is a mode of expression, must be distinguished from "the symbolic," which is the application of a "state of mind," or, again, a "mentality." Symbolism is technique; the symbolic is the form of writing of a vital philosophy.

Symbolic Modes

WHEN AN IMAGE, a collection of letters, a word or a phrase, a gesture, a single sound, a musical harmony or melody have a significance through *evocation*, we are dealing with a symbol.

This presupposes that the meaning of the determined aspect of the symbol must be known, so as to be able to evoke a non-determined aspect in the consciousness of the observer. This is the common nature of the symbol—somehow its rallying effect is like the effect that a few notes of a national anthem may have on patriots under an invader's yoke.

On the other hand, no one would understand the meaning of U.N., Y.M.C.A., U.S.S.R., etc., if the meaning of each juxtaposition of initials had not been explained. Once acknowledged, it evokes the groups it represents, fulfilling a rallying role. An image used as a trademark means nothing symbolically without a previous explanation.

On the contrary, a melody evokes moments experienced, producing gaiety or sadness, just as a symphony can transport the audience into a spring or autumn landscape. Here it is a matter of an emotive evocation, and the music is its symbol. In literature a metaphor is a symbol evoking a meaning by analogy; allegory is a symbol causing a play of the imagination which will replace the description given.

These are examples of *exoteric symbolism:* all the data—symbol and evocation—are objective or objectifiable.

The esoteric symbolic is different; it is of a magical nature.[1]

1. The word *magic* is understood here with the same sense as "magus" and not "magician." The Three Wise Men (Magi) of the Gospel and Hermes Trismegistus

For example, the grating produced by rubbing metal against a tin can set one's teeth on edge. In the same way a disharmony will make the listener start and cause him to feel uncomfortable. A caricature makes people laugh. "Medusa's image turned (the beholder) into stone." A roar in the silence of the forest will make the bravest person tremble; two phosphorescent eyes in the woods at night will create fear.

Such things may be analysed as the shock of the unexpected, effects of the imagination.

But the grating that sets one's teeth on edge is the effect neither of surprise nor of imagination; it is a constant effect. Similarly, the noise made by a trickle of water stimulates the need to urinate even when one is asleep. The repetition of the same monotonous sound (litanies) puts the mental consciousness to sleep. Manifold examples of the "magic of analogues," producing reactions at a distance, are esoteric symbolic effects. Untidy surroundings render the occupants dirty and slovenly. The environment is always a magical symbol. The highlander differs, in character and manners, from the lowlander. When the sailor accustomed to scanning the sky occasionally cultivates his land, he does so absolutely differently from the peasant who keeps his eyes to the ground.

The country makes the man; the sky makes the earth. Sky and earth are the great symbols that dominate humanity.

The esoteric symbol is a natural or artificial fact which elicits an abstract vital response, which will then be expressed physically, nervously, mentally, or emotionally in an organized being, or by an energetic reaction in a non-organized being.

The effect produced by the atmosphere of a cathedral—by its vaults, columns, stained glass windows, and figured sym-

---

are related to this true magic (creative magic) of spiritual action, at the right moment, in the right setting. This magic is the essence of Harmony, Justice, and Beauty. It concerns the magical effect and not the product, which may please or displease us. The magical effect can only be produced through a perfect accord between the nature of the Cause and its setting and the propitious moment.

bols of religious principles—is known. Thus, one could concede that if the symbolic is extended to the choice of the stones, the metals, the colors, the materials placed in the foundation, the favorably placed lights—if, in short, everything corresponds symbolically to the significance of the place—one could, I say, understand the magical effect of this symbolic, which is as nearly absolute as possible.

In literature only the parable represents the esoteric symbolic. It could be explained in terms of the effect of a parabolic mirror: all the parallel incident rays are reflected on a single central point, just as they are moreover, when focused by a biconvex lens.

But hieroglyphic writing is the ultimate esoteric symbolic writing, in the figuration of its signs as well as their color and placement.[2]

---

2. That I mention neither Heraldry nor Liturgy here is intentional. The introduction of these themes would require explanations too long for this short treatise.

Fig. 4. Nut, the Sky, swallows the sun each evening and brings it forth into the world again at dawn. The pattern on her dress evokes celestial waves, and particles of solar radiation innundate the face of Hathor, with the cow's ears, that rises at the horizon.

Symbol—Synthesis

THE WORD *symbol,* derived and distorted from its usual Greek meaning, signifying a sign of recognition or password, has become synonymous with the representation of a concept by a conventional sign. The assemblage of the parts of a broken potsherd, which could also be represented by a torn note or visiting card, meant—probably in a popular sense—the symbol or (hieroglyphic) sign of recognition.

Nowadays any letter or image that replaces the development of an idea is called a symbol (such as a chemical symbol for simple or composite bodies, or the initials of the words of a phrase to designate a group, or a speaking or representational figure for a trademark); but a single conventional letter in a mathematical operation (such as the coefficient Pi for the circle, h for Planck's constant, M for mass, c for the speed of light, etc.) is also called a symbol, as each letter requires a long development to explain its meaning, thus summarized.

Whether it is a natural or combined image, or a conventional sign, the *property of the symbol is to be a synthesis.*

When, in chemistry, one wished to represent a combination, one was led to specify the assemblage of the parts in a static two-or-three-dimensional form, and one had recourse to an image either in plane or in volume. These images are symbols—that is, syntheses—and not the true representation of the combination. They serve only as support (intuitively placed in the schema) of an essentially qualitative function which probably cannot be specified in Time and Space.

It is a property of thought to need a support, an hypothesis of a specific nature. This can be called an intuition-base, forming a scaffolding for the expression of knowledge through series and groups, implied ideas, atmosphere, analogies—in short, all the radiation stemming from this symbol–synthesis. Evolved thought, which is only an expansion of consciousness, then rids itself of the support. It could be said that *the abstract Spirit needs a concrete support, which, by its nature, must be the synthesis (located in Time and Space) of the form to be given to the Spirit so that it may have available the body necessary for experience. Later, this support is cast off, leaving the new concept in its purity.*

Synthesis should not be considered solely as a product of thought. In the chemical concrete sense of the word, nature offers syntheses. But it is above all in its psychological meaning that we should take this word. Here is what Kant had to say about it: "By the word *synthesis* in its most general signification, I understand the process of joining different representations to each other and of comprehending their diversity in one cognition."[1] To Kant's definition I should add that every natural thing is synthesis for rational science, which must proceed by analysis in order to acquire knowledge of the component parts or of the nature of the thing. Let me also add what Marcelin Berthelot understands by chemical synthesis, "that which can produce new combinations unknown to nature."

There are three types of syntheses and three types of symbols:

The vital synthesis—which is the natural symbol and its expression (tangible form, characteristic word or sound, and color)—is the pure *symbol*.

The action of synthesis, which represents the *pseudo-symbol* (such as the word, the vocable), replacing the image and determining the concept.

---

1. Emmanuel Kant, *Critique of Pure Reason*, trans. J.M.D. Meiklejohn, book 1, section 3.

The synthesizing effect of thought, or psychological synthesis, which represents the para-symbol, through the conventional symbol summarizing a thought.

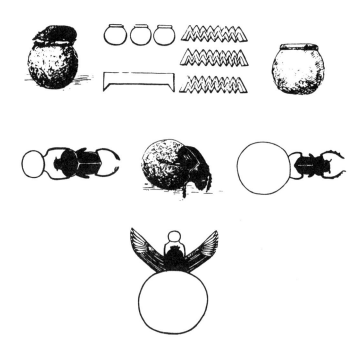

Fig. 5. Top row: The sacred scarab preparing to lay its eggs — its sheep-dung ball in the form of the Nw vase. The hieroglyph of the Nw vase is used to write, among other things, Nw, "the primordial waters;" Nw.t, "the scarab's own ball in which are brought about its metamorphoses;" Nw.t, "Time." Middle row: The sacred scarab, the only insect that manufactures a perfect sphere which it rolls with its back legs and buries in the ground. Lower row: Winged scarab rises up from a sphere rolling the symbol of the rising sun with its front legs.

All these aspects of synthesis are the *symbols* of the set of functions, as well as the assemblage of parts that the synthesis implies.

Thus, the symbol serves equally well for the objectification of thought as for a system of references; but in its esoteric sense it will act as psychological synthesis evoking the functions, thus the unobjectifiable qualitative relationships that its specific form synthesizes.

Today the new scientific thought should clearly call upon two forms of intelligence, since experiment and observation require a determinist stance in Time and Space, manifesting, at the same time, the indeterminable aspect of the simultaneity imposed by the phenomenon.[2] It could be said, for the objective intelligence, there is a past and a future but *never a Present* and that, for Reality, there is an eternal, invariable Present, outside of Time.[3]

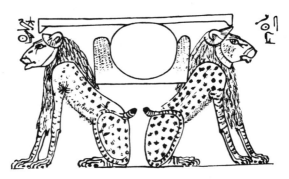

Fig. 6. The sun at the horizon between the two Aker lions called "Yesterday" and "Tomorrow." The commentary on this image reads, "To me belongs yesterday and I know tomorrow. What is this? Yesterday is Osiris, tomorrow is Re." (Papyrus of Ani, Chapter 17).

2. This state of simultaneity, absurd yet logical, can be interpreted mathematically by the root of minus one ($\sqrt{-1}$) which can only be $+1$ and simultaneously -1, or ± 1.

3. See the chapter, "The Principle of the Present Moment."

One may opt for either of these considerations. Each can be relatively *true*. But what matters is not a relative truth, but what is real, and by this word I mean that which is invariable. In this sense the symbol does not have to be true, nor to be considered as such; it is not the truth, but it is the "reality." It is objectively determined in Time and Space, but, as simultaneity (synthesis), it is outside of Time. The symbol as synthesis is the eternal "Present Moment," because the same conjunction of conditions that created its development will compel it continually to be what it is; this prescribes the notion of identity, which is objectively inconceivable.

There is a reversal of positions for the two intelligences: for the objective intelligence, there is determinism, where for the unexpressed, intuitive intelligence (innate knowledge) there is non-determinism. On the other hand, the non-determinism of simultaneity for the objective intelligence becomes the deter-mined reality for the unformulated, intuitive intelligence.

To explain the preceding, let us take the example of the coefficient Pi. Objectively, the circle is comprehensible only as an assemblage of the bases of triangles having their apexes at the center of the circle (Euclid). Thus, one will attempt to calculate the coefficient of its ratio to its diameter by means of polygons and by an estimate resulting from the inscribed and circumscribed polygons.

It is evident that one will never get a finite number in this way, and Pi must be an irrational number. One accepts the "absurd" formula of a polygon with an *infinite* number of sides, which attests to the *feeling* that the circle can in no way be known through polygons: intuitively, we are certain that the circle is a line that is curved along every part of its path, however small that part may be. For instance, let us make an object describe a circle: it is evident that only an indefinable, immaterial moment (as an extension of the radius tracing this circle) will follow the curve, while the object, in its length, will always be only tangent.

The letter Pi, chosen arbitrarily, becomes a symbol. As a symbol, this Pi *synthesizes* an objectively incomprehensible, inexplicable function, and every mathematical effort to calculate this value must, at each moment, call upon an abstract reality, intuitively known and objectively inexpressible. This is the case for all mathematical symbols and ultimately for the symbol in general. The symbol Pi is a synthesis; the symbol c is the synthesis of the speed of light; in Egyptian *hieroglyphs*, the cubit (the forearm) is the *symbol of the synthesis of measurements*, because of its measure of the universe particularized in the human microcosm, but it is not a defined measurement.[4]

Fig. 7. "I am this pure lotus which emerges carrying the luminous . . ." cry the dead (alluding to the Hermopolitan myth in which the sun is born from the calyx of a lotus rising up from the waters), ". . . everything takes birth through him, the child (who shines) in the lotus whose rays give life to all beings."

4. In this connection let us recall that in China there is, for the measurement of the human body, a measure (a small measure) called *tsun* which is on the one hand, peculiar to each individual and, moreover, different for the head, the limbs, and the trunk. It is indispensable to know these units of measurement for acupuncture and for studying pulses.

Let us also note that every unit of measure of length is called "tsun." Similarly, in Egypt the "cubit" unit has several meanings which one can only understand if one knows the philosophy of its application.

The symbol acts as the link between the rational intelligence and the intelligence today called surrational; the latter can only be expressed in mathematical form. We are dealing here with a new consciousness, that is, epistemologically speaking, a new state of the power of thought; this seems to have been known to and evident among the Ancient Egyptians, since they constructed all their expression on the knowledge of this dualism of intelligence, which tradition labels Exotericism and Esotericism.

The ordinary consideration of the Egyptian symbol reduces it to a primary arbitrary, utilitarian, and singular meaning, whereas in reality it is a synthesis which requires great erudition for its *analysis* and a special culture for the esoteric knowledge that it implies—which does not exclude the necessity of being "simple" or knowing how to "simply look" at the symbol.

Innate Knowledge Summary

EACH TIME an activity and its consequent reactions have produced a phenomenon exhausting all the energies involved, this phenomenon counts as One; that is, it constitutes an individuality. Egyptian calculation proceeds in this way by fractions, as do our mathematics as well. In relation to a new function, the symbol counts as One.

Thus, the symbol is the characteristic principle of Pythagorean number: there is the "enumerating number" and the "enumerable number" of ordinary arithmetic and the non-enumerable number of the Science of Numbers, the new Unity, an entity derived from the "vital connection" of the component numbers and not from a quantitative addition.

There is, for example, a trunk and its branches, constituting a tree. This tree, as such, has new qualities; it is a whole, a new individual. In another category, one can also say that a bouquet is a whole which represents what each of the flowers composing it cannot be separately.

We count five fingers, and this number, five, is no longer an addition of five units, but a *hand* with new qualities and a particular power which none of the single fingers can have. Thus, in the Pythagorean sense, each number is a unity in itself, an entity, an individuality, and as such it is nonenumerable.

This principle of grouping has become an important factor in the new scientific thought. One no longer speaks of the Pythagorean Number, but its principle is applied.[1] All the

1. This is said without taking into account the mathematical nature of the new scientific thought. The manner in which one succeeds in finally conceiving the universe,

56

events in time, nondeterminable for the isolated individual, show themselves—in the totality of the groupings of these individuals—to be independent with respect to one another. The greater their number, the more precise becomes the calculation of probability. The inability of exoteric (objective) intelligence to study the secret of the life of the individual in any depth drives the microphysicist, as well as the sociologist, to address the principle of collectivity in order to derive statistical conclusions. This "lure" is a last resource, pending the time when the reality of the "other intelligence," that which might be called "innate knowledge," is recognized.[2]

The statistical conclusion, useful for the collectivity, is an error in terms of the individual. *The group is "a whole," a new being;* its energy is new; its tendencies are different from those of the units that constitute it. Therefore, after research on the atom, it will be necessary to return to the study of the complex (the group) in order to know the simple, since—*with the rational, scientific method*—the simple is impenetrable.

In our symbolic approach it is understood that the individual is itself composed of a group, but through this group it has become an individuality, that is, a unity independent from other similar unities. Thus, each part of what composes it can no longer be regarded as an individuality and can no longer even be objectified. Thus, one may only speak of

---

expressed by mathematical values, has nothing in common with Pythagorean number, no more than do the "matrix forms," or forms defined by coordinates of surface or volume. At most one can "prophesy" that the new thought will end up concluding, along with the Pythagorean school, that the Universe is nothing but Number.

2. In this connection, see Lecomte du Noùy, *L'Homme devant la science* (Paris: Flammarion, 1941) p. 207. "We have seen that, despite the flexibility that the possibility of fluctuations confers on them, the laws of large numbers (calculation of probabilities) do not succeed in providing us with any plausible or probable explanation for the phenomenon of Life. Determinism does not even tackle these problems, for it is not, and has never been, a constructive tool, and it cannot, in any case, explain an evolution, whatever it may be. Like the calculation of probabilities, it recognizes only one motive force: chance. But it makes this chance intervene only once, at the origin of the universe. And everything that follows is the ineluctable consequence of this first throw of the dice, the flick of the hand for which Pascal could not forgive Descartes."

qualitative or energetic "Principles."[3]

The vital experience of the individuality becomes its own and can only affect the principles of its constitution. It is this modification, introduced into the energetic whole constituting the individuality, that specifies the latter; the vital experience modifies its *specification* in a constant manner, constituting its acquired experience, which then alone will influence the genes and their mutation—will create what I call the "cerebrally unconscious consciousness" or *innate knowledge.*

Thanks to this innate consciousness we are able to *understand;* it is the Intellect, or living soul, that sensorial observation—through evocation—will cause to create.

3. The *Neter* (plural: *Neteru*) is principle, but is not used as a word signifying "the principle" in ancient Egypt. *Neter* is clumsily translated as "God," which, in Judeo-Christian deism, has the connotation of an absolute Unity. The Greek "daimon" would be more suitable. But why not simply say "Neter"?

The Principle of the Present Moment

TIME IS measured by movement. At each instant a movement can only be completed or about to start. It cannot be otherwise, as it cannot be past and future "at the same time." The Present Moment cannot therefore be situated: it is outside of Time, because it is outside of measurable movement. It presents the conditions of an Absolute.

It is from this Absolute that we constantly draw our forces. In dying the cell reproduces itself. This passage from One to Two is its "Present Moment," which cannot be located in Time, although the phases of karyokinesis succeed one another to create the genesis of the new cell. The "Present Moment" is "that which compels the nucleus to divide."

Each instant of life is negation and affirmation "at the same time," that is, absence of Time. We can, by extension, speak of a duration as being the *present* hour or epoch, for example. But each moment of this hour or epoch is a "collision" between the impulsion of the past and the obstacle of the future.

It is only by locating ourselves outside of Time that we can speak of a Presence. For example, a given person is present: he is not elsewhere; he is here, in a specific space—that is, a movement arrested in Time. Thus, Presence belongs to the past and not to the future. This is illustrated, for example, by the "Royal Presence," symbolized in the British Parliament by the "Mace." This is a stop in Time, like a milestone on the road, which does not prevent Time from passing beside it or the road from unwinding.

Presence is a symbol; the Present Moment is Eternity.

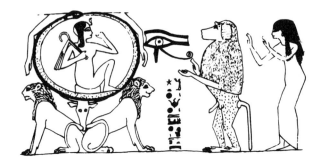

Fig. 8. From right to left: the singer of Amun, Her-Ouben, and the baboon of Thoth in front of the Oudja eye, under which is inscribed "Adoration to Re, new year of Re, in the barque of Re in the sky." Between the two Aker-lions (Yesterday and Tomorrow), above an antelope head, Horus the Child (Horus Harpocrate), wearing the braid of the crown prince and with his finger at his lip, is seated on the sign of the horizon inside the solar disk which is in turn encircled by the serpent who bites his own tail (symbol of eternity) and is itself embraced by two arms descending from heaven.

The Discontinuous Object in the Continuous Present

IN THE vital phenomenon, genesis is the dynamic aspect.[1] A given moment of the functional relationships that constitute genesis is the vital moment. One can know the vital moment only when it is stopped by death; this is its static moment, which signifies its negation. Thus, one cannot know this vital moment objectively: one can only know its effects—that is, its *fixed* effects, the stages of genesis.

The objective awareness of "dynamic-static" simultaneity is impossible, since there is a contradiction; but it is possible using the intuitive (unexpressed) intelligence, of the vital dynamism, to juxtapose or compare the objective symbol with the static (located) state of the vital moment, its current stage.

This state of comparison—that is, of juxtaposition of an objective state, unstable in Time, with an ever-present state of simultaneity—should not be confused with the juxtaposition of two worlds, or two "presences." In the Present everything mingles, including all the instants of the genesis of every thing. The Present is an unobjectifiable dimension which contains all volumes. From the point of view of Space, it is *Necessity* that compels things to exist under specific conditions; it is also, in the sense of Time, the *Possibility* immanent in each object at each instant. Thus, Creation is constant for esotericism, but for exotericism it is located: "In the beginning . . ."

1. Here the word *dynamic* is used in the sense of an exhausted impulsion which engenders a vital succession, or genesis, and not in the kinematic sense of a displacement in space.

The unexpressed awareness of simultaneity is synthesis, and not synthesizing; it is the esoteric meaning, whereas exotericism is necessarily analytic.

The opinion of Science (which I consider erroneous) is that Knowledge will be achieved through the synthesis of analytically located elements, but, I think that—just as one can glimpse in mathematics—with the expansion of consciousness our thought is heading toward "direct synthetic vision."

In this sense, the symbol is thus the object, exterior to us, which awakens innate knowledge through the senses. This creates our intuitive knowledge of the simultaneous, a continuity in which a discontinuity is located.

For example, the image of a bird in flight is the symbol of the flight of a winged animal. This image is a static moment (arrested in Time) of this function of flying, its fixation. This symbol arouses in us not only what we have registered in our memory concerning the flight of birds, but also our innate knowledge of flight, *our sensation of flight,* and we embody this knowledge in the image-symbol, which thus becomes a synthesis of *our* knowledge of the flight of the bird. What matters is not the image but the symbol-synthesis of the function of the vital moment.

The image is death; the symbol is life. In relation to life, death is nothing but a fixation in Time, hence a false eternity. True eternity must be sought in the innate, unexpressed, consciousness which becomes the intuitive knowledge of simultaneity.

Now, one would have to be omniscient to be able to discern all the possibilities contained in a symbol, which would imply the "innate knowledge" of the entire Universe.

Consequently, in order to make practical use of the symbol, a system consisting in a choice of the possibilities that should be looked for in it would appear inevitable. But to attempt to set up a rational system (which is possible, if need be) would be to fall back into an exoteric interpretation which would deprive the symbol of the possibility of speaking esoterically.

The choice should be made by the reader, solely in the light of and to the extent of his own innate knowledge.

One need only note the philosophic principles to which the symbols conform in order to learn then to seek in oneself the summary meaning of their synthesis.

One must also know that, for example, in ancient Egypt the choice of an animal as a symbol was guided by a profound knowledge of the life of that animal, of its vital characteristics, its habits, its assimilation, the length of its gestation, its mating customs (the season and even the time of day), etc.[2] *In the doctrine of the microcosm, each animal is a stage in the universal gestation, the goal of which, for us, is Man: Homo sapiens.*

Fig. 9. "I am this Phoenix which is at Heliopolis! . . . What is this? . . . It is eternity and perpetuity . . ." (Papyrus of Ani, Chapter 17). At the end of the innundation recalling the primordial waters, Nu, dryness appears, (oubenn) in the form of the first hillock, and the ash-colored heron, the benu bird, glides majestically down and rests on the benn-benn stone at Heliopolis. The recurrence of this phenomenon gave birth to the legend of the Phoenix reborn from its own ashes, thus symbolizing perpetuity (Pyramid Texts, 1652).

2. The Egyptian symbolic does not hesitate to choose, among all the varieties of a type, the characteristic elements that one wishes to accentuate, thus creating a composite image, which our scholars attempt tirelessly—and in vain—to place in a schematic classification.

Relationship Is The Symbol of Being

BEING, AS existence, manifests only through relationship, that is, the interchange between the two component complements of Being.

We call complements the two specific qualities of a thing, one of which denies the other.

For instance, brightness and shadow make light. Without shadow, no object would be visible, so that if brightness were without shadow, we should no more know light than does a blind man. This proposition can also be reversed: the blind man is he who lives in a brightness without shadow—which is often true.

Another widely known example is that of complementary colors, such as red and green, yellow and purple, orange and blue. Superimposed, by means of subtraction, these complements annul all color, and (theoretically) make black; added together, they (theoretically) give white light.

Complements do not exist separately, any more than does the North Pole without the South Pole; they are the abstract components of Being; they are, essentially, the active and passive, male and female principles.[1]

The mechanical passive state, which is merely a lesser activity, should not be confused with the vital passive principle.

In the vital state, the complements are the poles of a single axis and not a relative state, as would be the relationship of

1. The Chinese *yin* and *yang*.

Fig. 10. At the center is the double head of Seth of the South and Horus of the North; it emerges from a single body standing on the falcon-headed lion that wears the white crown of the South. On his hindquarters is a human head, also wearing the white crown. To the right and to the left are stakes, each surmounted by a head crowned with the white crown; the stakes lean severely, as if repelled by the central image and pulled in the opposite direction by the two groups of snake-headed personages wearing the crowns of the North and of the South that symbolize the blind forces, positive and negative, of the terrestrial magnetism.

two objects moving at different speeds. *The passive principle is an inverse activity.*[2]

There is an interchange of activities, an exchange of energy; hence, the possibility of addition and subtraction, of mutual annihilation or exaltation. This *relationship* is thus the symbol of Being: the thing.

The symbol links complements, demonstrates Being, implies the positive and negative activities; it is the transient, phenomenal aspect between the causal abstraction and its negation.

Thus, the symbol must always be considered as a *relationship* between two abstract and complementary elements.

For example, the hare is not a symbol for the hunter, because he considers the hare in relation to other game: foxes, partridges, quails.

2. In this connection, let us note that the Spirit, or formless substance, is passive. This is the cosmic feminine principle. It is through the effect of *odor* which is the "acting verb" that this "word," through femininity, falls into nature. (For a definition of "odor" see p. 74.)

The hare can only be a symbol in relationship to itself, that is, as the resultant of the vital data which is "specifically hare." Consequently, the same food will produce a hare in its case, a rabbit in the case of the rabbit. *To be a hare* means above all, to be a specific ferment that transforms all energy it receives into hare (for instance, by the air breathed and the solid and liquid food). For this reason, all the physical and psychic characteristics, as well as the activities of this hare, will be manifest in this symbol. The hare-symbol, as a relationship between the principles of its specific seed, is a typal phase, located embryologically (in the cosmic sense) within the development of the ultimate being toward which Nature tends. Its image can thus express the entire complex of this phase, and a nuance in this figuration can accentuate a principle of particular note.

The Crossing: Principle of Evocation

EVERY CAUSE must be considered as an activity which is relatively positive or negative.

The phenomenal consequence of the cause is always "cathodic," because, without resistance, the reabsorption of the causal activity would only be an annulment, and because resistance necessarily causes a reaction.

The cathodic effect is the best illustration of the reactive effect, as is shown by the effect of reflection in a Crook's cathode tube.[1] Thus, the light of the moon can be considered a cathodic effect—that is, an effect *embodying* the rays of the sun. A similar, special effect is produced on each planet; the intensity of the solar flux and the nature of the cathode, as well as the angle of reflection, modify the resulting radiation. The "embodying" character of the cathode signifies the specification of the neutral incident radiation.

Every cause—or, more correctly, every activity—is a cause only because of the opposed and *reacting* resistance. This reaction is a "phenomenon." Neither the emission of the anode nor the obstacle of the cathode appear in the empty tube. The Roentgen ray that results from them is a phenomenon, and we now know that it is a question of a truly new activity (reactivity) of the atoms of the cathode.

---

1. The positive current of an induction current (static electricity) is introduced, by means of an "anode" into a tube that has been made a vacuum as much as possible. Opposite this "anode" is the "cathode," which catches the negative current and contains a sort of mirror (metallic foil) placed at an angle of 45°, so as to reflect the positive current caught toward one side of the tube. Once outside the tube, this flux (in the case x-rays) is the cathodic effect.

This principle of reactivity is applied in the esoteric symbolic. It is prescribed by the fact that an intellectual (unsituated) definition is impossible. Thus, this definition must *be evoked* by reaction, but one cannot describe it without locating it in Time and Space, hence "fixing" it.

The symbol, as synthesis evokes—through its static and concrete nature—the functional and qualitative whole from which it arises; that is, it vitally evokes its nonlocatable definition.

This mode of thought is the key to pharaonic thinking.[2] It is also moreover, similar to that of the Chinese.[3]

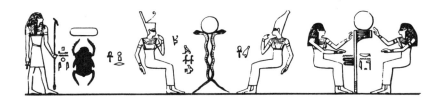

Fig. 11. "They are thus in the Dwat (the netherworld) as forms and births of Khepri when he carries his oval (Nw.t) towards this place, in order to then come forth at the eastern horizon of the sky . . ."
"These Neteru *are thus the left (eye) coming out of the interlaced double right (eye) coming out of* sdfy.t *" (the symbol of the Neter). (Amdwat, 10th hour). At the left the scarab carries not a ball, but a characteristic cocoon (Nw.t), containing the pupa of a butterfly or moth. At the right, the right eye or solar glove rises out of the symbol of the divine. At the center, the crossing of the serpents evokes conjunction at the bottom and opposition at the top, the principle phases of the left, lunar eye.*

2. See the chapter, "The Symbolic."

3. Marcel Granet, "La Pensée Chinoise," in *L'Evolution de l'humanites* (Renaiseance du Livre).
    This is also the principle of the "homeopathic" method of therapeutics.

The Symbol as Expression of a Will

EVERY CIRCLE, as a circular movement, has a center. This center controls this continuous and regular curve, which is closed; it is attractive, just as the circumference is repellent (centrifugal). This center is an abstract power which rules the phenomenon of circular movement. Two centers make an elliptical (or assimilated) movement if the curve is closed. If the curve is not closed but is superimposed, the center becomes a line or a figure, horizontal for a spiral, vertical for a helicoidal curve, etc.

The center controls; it is the *will of the figure*. Three axes of equal length, intersecting at 90°, are the *will* of the cube. The form of the movement and the form of the Euclidean volume are in the center and in its radiation.

I say that the *will* of a rotating sphere is the magnetic axis, and its equator is the centrifugal electrical effect. On the other hand, every magnetic effect is contracting *will*, which produces the dilating, equatorial electrical effect. Inversely, every circular electrical current provokes the magnetic axial effect. Will is esoteric; effect is exoteric.

But where, then, is the will of the "container," the non-Euclidean volume?

Its will is the seed, that is, the specification of the "contents," hence a genesis—that is, Time, for Time is none other than genesis. Genesis appears to us as Time.

Now, all will of movement and of form is a specification of Energy. Will is thus identified with the seed, as the *specifier*, and, as genesis, appears as Time or duration.

The seed ordains the volume, that is, Space; the genesis of this Space ordains Time. Will is what Lao-Tzu calls "the empty hub of the wheel."[1]

The Absolute Will of the Origin includes all specifications.

Everything that is naturally specified is a symbol and the expression of a will, hence of a specifying seed of non-objectifiable Energy: the Container, the non-polarized Spirit-substance. The specifying Will, the "Fire" of the seed, was called the "odor" by ancient Egyptians—the "odor" of the *Neter*, (that is, in an esoteric sense, that which is emanated by the Neter like an ejaculated seed).

The contained will must always be sought in the symbol, when the symbol is selected for an esoteric teaching. The character of this Will is that which will always compel Spirit—non-polarized Energy—to define itself in Time and Space, hence in the *form* of the symbol. This is the "magical" meaning of the symbol. With regard to Spirit, this "magic" operates like the Platonic Idea, just as rhythm acts on our will of movement; we obey despite and at odds with everything, even when we do not give in.

1. In the *Tao Te Ching*, Lao-Tzu, the splendid sage, says (roughly): "The wheel has twelve spokes which meet at the center. Neither the rim nor the spokes make the wheel; it is the empty hub that makes the wheel."

The Symbolic

THE SYMBOLIC is the means of expression—the form of writing—of "vitalist" philosophy; the symbol is its vital synopsis.

Since, as we have seen, the symbol is the static form of the relationship between two moments which are incomprehensible in their simultaneity, the juxtaposition of symbols makes possible the expression—without formulation—of identities of nature which can manifest in opposing dualities.

It is evident that in a vitalist philosophy the symbol should act as the concept. But this concept has value only through the idea implied, since it is merely the relationship between this idea and its complement. The symbol is thus the synopsis of a logical function, rather than a concept which fits into a quantitative syllogistic function.

This philosophy is that of the vital and "non-quantitative" play, that is, it relates functions only and not factors, and thus it cannot include an equational play of syllogism, for which the data (even when abstract) are rendered through comparison, objectifiable. For instance, "karyokinesis" is in itself a non-objectifiable function. It is objectifiable only in its static moments and not in its vital, dynamic moment. The essence of this function is the scission of a unity: the resulting duality confirms this for us. It is not this duality which is the scission: *as will, this scission is identical to the original scission, or Creation,* but it is distinguishable from the latter by the fact that it works on something that is qualitatively divisible. In every function there is this moment which cannot be located in

Fig. 12. At the right, we see the barque in which the ram-headed scarab rows, framed by the souls of Tum (the demiurge) and Kephri (the scarab, "becoming"). The barque descends down the back of Aker, the lion, and is received by Ta-tenen, Memphite entity of "the earth-which-emerges." Between the two groups of three mummiform personages called "the waters of Nu," two arms rise up supporting the solar globe. At the left, it is Nu, himself, who makes the boat ascend on the back of the lion Aker for its daily reappearance.

Time; I call it the "Present Moment." It is this *esoteric* moment that the symbolic is concerned with, and in it the symbol acts as the synopsis which conveys this implied functional idea. The only way we will ever know this non-definable idea is through the certainty of our innate knowledge, which assures us of this reality which is *necessarily implied* in the symbol. For instance, if a stone falls, this fact implies an attraction which we do not know in itself; we know it only through a juxtaposition of the quantitative elements of an analysis that can be formulated into laws. We may speak of a mass that attracts, but this tells us no more about what this attraction is.

The falling of the stone is an esoteric symbol, if we consider it in terms of the implied idea, but if we regard this fall as being situated in Time and Space, it is only an exoteric fact, from a quantitative knowledge. Now, it is the "function of that which attracts" that is cosmic reality, and not the attraction itself, which only acts as such within a certain aspect of matter, *as microphysics has recently revealed.*

Thus, vital philosophy, expressed by the symbolic, is concerned with the eternal vital moment and not its accidental applications, in which it can always modify its appearance.

Under these conditions, can one reason—that is, construct a system of *vital logic?* Certainly, if one does not seek a conclusion arrested in Time and Space. It is Life—dynamism in itself—that matters; the revelation of the symbol, then, is universal. This means that there is no difference in the vital moment with respect to the condition in which it manifests. For example, if a given plant is an aphrodisiac for a bull, there is in this plant the same functional state (one may recall the Arcana of Paracelsus) as that which, for the bull, causes its sexual irritation. There is a functional identity. Moreover, if this plant (a static moment or a symbol in the Universe) exists and likewise the bull exists (or even if this bull no longer exists), the reality (or Idea) of this plant *is, was,* and always *will be;* it corresponds to a phase of the cosmic genesis that will persevere, because of the fact of constant creation.

Herein lies a basis for the solution of the problem of original causality.

When, through analysis, one arrives at the energetic origin of matter, one can dispute *the principle of original causality* insofar as one persists in seeing in the phenomenon only a quantitative sequence, and as long as life is viewed as a bio-physico-chemical (and today, of course, microphysical) effect. The borderline is pushed back; it is not crossed. This reduces the "cause" in general to a dynamic effect of quantity, a dynamic caused by the very nature of the energetic constitution of the atom. In this case, one sees in Energy only a polarized Energy, that is, an energetic *effect,* and no longer an original cause.

Einstein defines energy as an effect of Mass and of the speed of its motion;[1] therefore there is mass and there is

1. This speed is a limit qua c^2 or the speed of light squared. Therefore, the mass $M = Ec^2$.

motion; therefore there is also Time and Space (whatever sub-
terfuge one uses to disengage oneself from them) even if this
mass is a state of Energy.

Could one conceive science without a system of reference?
That would be a *Fiat Lux*, hence a cause outside of the system.

The problem that we thought was definitely eliminated
again arises today, for now we find ourselves facing an impasse.
We resolve the difficulty by acknowledging that everything is,
ultimately, light—the ultimate system of reference: c = the
speed of the propagation of light. Now, is light a cause? If so,
in what does it act? And if it is an effect, what is its cause?

Insofar as we have not acknowledged the reality of the
"Present," not accepted this moment which is incomprehensible in the phenomenal world, but which imposes itself even
on the rational—insofar as we have not accepted the principle
of the eternity of the Present, the necessity for a duality,
Science and Belief, remains; and "historians," in their interpretation of tradition, are, to a certain extent, right to distrust
"symbolism."

This notion of the eternal Present requires certain specifications.

Exoterically we foresee that, under certain conditions, a
given cause will produce a given result. All knowledge is based
on this foresight which is the result of observation and constitutes a primary determinism. This empiricism makes possible
the generalization that formulates the laws of science.

Now, philosophically, a cause is only Cause at the moment
it produces an effect, which is in no way certain. Under the
same known conditions, the same cause may happen to
produce a very different effect. For instance, we know today
that influences (such as that of cosmic rays) can modify the
effect of a chemical reaction.

Let us suppose that a stone falls from the cornice of a
house. It is too late to warn the passer-by that this stone is
about to kill him. We know that this stone is going to kill this

man; we foresee this effect. What foresees? Our memory; it shows us the inevitability of this effect. The inevitability is in our imagination which is created by our memory. For, in reality, this stone may be diverted from its course; the man may move a little faster or more slowly and the stone will miss him. In any event, the falling stone will only be the cause of the crushing of this passer-by (and hence will only produce its effect) if it finds in this man an obstacle to its fall. Before this point, it is not the cause.

Cause and effect are not separated by any time. No chemical reaction can liberate the elements during the moment of their passage from one combination to another. Often it is gaseous bodies that *pass* thus, and no traces prove their existence in the free state.[2] Indeed, just as in biology, in the conjunction of the spermatazoon with the nucleus of the ovum,[3] as well as in the crystallization of a salt, the chemical reaction takes place outside of Time. There are, in the world, effects; but the distance in time between cause and effect does not exist. All creation is constant in the eternal Present. Now, fertilization—that is, the vital moment of the conjunction— obeys the law of Creation; it is instantaneous, as is, for example, the appearance of a crystal in its mother liquid solution. The same is true of the conjunction of chemical elements. It is

2. The following objections may be raised: (1) the inertia of matter; (2) the fact that chemical reaction takes place more rapidly under the effect of heat (in this connection see Van't Hoff's law). In the opposite direction, thermodynamics shows that at absolute zero (–273°), all chemical reaction must cease. Heat thus intervenes as a factor in the reaction by dispersing (liquifying) the molecular medium, facilitating the reaction, but temperature in no way modifies its nature. Whether the reaction takes place rapidly or slowly, the Present Moment of the "passage" cannot be located in Time.

3. Fertilization comprises the following phenomena:
    a. Attraction of the spermatazoa by the ova;
    b. penetration by the spermatazoon, formation of a defensive membrane, contraction of the protoplasm, and formation of a liquid between the two;
    c. *division* of the center of the spermatazoon into two centrosomes, *before* the conjunction of the two pronuclei;
    d. *conjunction* of the two pronuclei, while the two centrosomes separate;
    e. *immediate division of the new nucleus* (each group of its chromosomes is attracted by one of the centrosomes).

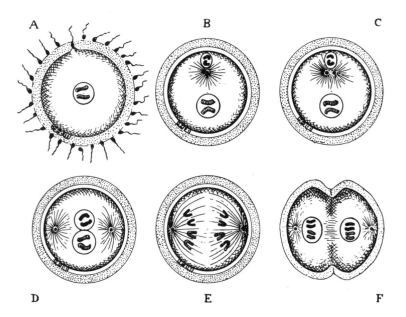

Fig. 13. Cellular Mitosis. Fecundation comprises the following phenomena: attraction of the spermatozoids by the ovules; penetration of the spermatozoid, the formation of a defense membrane, the contraction of the protoplasm, and the formation of a liquid between the two; the division of the spermocenter into two centrasomes before the conjunction of the two pronuclei; the conjunction of the two pronuclei while the two centrasomes separate. Each group of chromosomes is attracted by one of the centrosomes.

always a question in this case (that is of the relation between cause and effect) of a vital moment, which, even in inorganic matter, obeys the universal law of Creation: the *unformed substance receives form*, for it is always a matter of an activity balanced by an opposite activity, and activity signifies "dynamism in itself" before becoming a dynamic body. The effect is a neutralization of an activity, and this neutralization never occurs without the phenomenal reaction of resistance; it is simply a *chain* of activities, reaction being but a new activity of the first effect, hence the new cause. It is this "chain" which seems to us to be located in Time and Space, whereas *it*

Fig. 14. "Those who carry the intertwined double cord from which the stars come out." Thus are designated the twelve persons who extract the double cord from the mouth of Aken. Knowing that at each hour a star is born, we can understand the rest of the text which says that at each new twist, an hour is born, then, after the passage of the Great Neter, Aken reswallows the cord (thus making time go backwards). (Book of Gates, *5th division*).

is a gestation which is Time; but between Cause and Effect there exists no Time.[4]

The principle of the "Present Moment" is not a mystic doctrine, but it is a fact which has a mystical character.

This can be better understood through the image of the axis. Every body revolving about itself turns around an axis. The tangential projection of a diameter from the plane at right angles to this axis is contradictory at the opposite extremities.

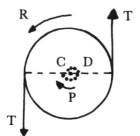

C—center, pole of the axis
D—diameter
T—tangential projection
R—direction of rotation
P—precessional motion

View, through the pole, of the plan
at right angles to the axis.

4. Let us note by this explanation that Time thus becomes a quantity in "duration" through the juxtaposition of parts, a kind of granulation. It is these "parts" or "quantities" which are the symbols of the universe and constitute a chain which has an apparent (objective) *beginning* and an end.

At the center—that is, on the axis—this projection is thus canceled, which would impose immobility on this center. To compensate for this impossibility, the axial pole is displaced and moves in the direction opposite that of the rotation, creating the precessional motion.[5]

If one could mechanically *impose* this immobility on this axial center during the rotation of the body, a disaggregation of the matter would necessarily follow once a certain speed had been reached.

The axis, called "an imaginary line," is actually "a fact of a mystical character": it exists and nevertheless remains exoterically incomprehensible; it is not the abstraction of a concrete datum; on the other hand, it is impossible to define whether it is effect or cause.

If now we consider the symbolic as being constructed with the symbol conceived as an apparent, transitory phenomenon connecting complements (that is, abstractions) unifying in a Present the discontinuity of the appearance in the continuity of this Present, then the symbolic no longer contradicts the historic fact, and the historic fact appears as *the exoteric character of an esoteric reality.* Now, it is reality alone that has a value, which is ineluctable, invariable.

In exotericism one never demonstrates the cause outside of the system except *with* the system, hence in a duality, one of whose poles is left to faith.

The symbol demonstrates the esotericism which, by means of the symbolic, unifies that which is divided and puts an end to the problem of causality. The cause, apparently outside of the system, is in it, eternally united and present, and creation is constant. Such-and-such a phenomenon *was* not; it *is* always *in our innate knowledge,* from which our consciousness increasingly expands with experience.

---

5. This is my own explanation and in no way corresponds with the "mechanistic" explanation which is given for the precessional motion.

Thus, light bears within itself that which acts and that in which it acts: the discontinuous within the continuous.

Light is, for true Light (the Genesis of Moses), the symbol of the Presence that is absolute Cause-Effect. Succession—that is, Time, as the distance between cause and effect—is a mental illusion and not a reality. This Time is inconceivable, so why imagine it? Cause cannot be cause without producing an effect, which will be a new cause under the conditions suitable for its activity. Thus, there may be, in the sensorial appearance, a sequence of effects but never a sequence from cause to effect. Time as genesis—or genesis as Time—moves in the direction of the effect becoming the new cause. Thus, the march of Time is irreversible. These are the dates of the cosmic genesis, the phases of which are the effects (the static vital moment), as the symbols—or "things"—subsist as individualities which exhaust themselves, *being finished as types* and no longer acting as causes.

Between the extreme original cause and the ultimate final cause (which one would like to call effect) is the phenomenon, world, of which we know—in different types of form—all the "static moments," that is, the momentary corpses that people the Universe. *These are the symbols of the evolution of Consciousness*—that is, of Thought—through all experiences. This is but actualized knowledge of one's "Self," still latent in the accident of the "Me."

There can only be one way in this despite the multitude of branchings. The goal is single, there is only one Reality, and the wildest, most scattered little branches send their sap to this heart.

As the principle of the function is unique, there is necessarily a relationship and an analogy between the moments of the great cosmic cycles and the small events on earth. For instance, we may find ourselves astronomically in the place of Aries (in the precessional cycle) and the event of earth can traverse all twelve signs 2,160 times. The influence of the

"Arian vital moment" will operate during each terrestrial vital moment of each sign, in Libra as well as in Leo, etc., coloring the Libra or Leo moment with its Aries temperament.[6]

Secondary, tertiary, or even more distant (branched) events—that is, "the historic"—cannot be independent of the symbolic of the moment. They become the symbol, the static synthesis-moment of cosmic life.

It is this life of the symbol (its esotericism) *identifying with this life,* that is Reality; it enables *that which was,* as a cosmic and historical event, actually to persist in us *from this moment forward* because the life of the symbol is the experience of our consciousness: the Consciousness of the human Microcosm, summarized by the cosmic Man, *through whom* we are all jointly bound.

And if this consciousness is particular for each person (since each individual, according to his faculties, may or may not recognize in it the state of the moment) it remains nonetheless universal, *present,* just as a universal container can hold all forms, just as the light-synthesis can offer all appearances.[7]

For esotericism, a problem of original causality does not exist.

Nature, on the other hand, is the world of the Creature; everything in it is dualized in its appearance, which is cerebrally perceptible for us. This is the exoteric world, the world which, for us, is outside of ourselves, "objective." Thus, as long as God and the Devil—popularly expressed—exist for us, in their extreme aspects, neither one is *real,* although they are relatively true.

6. This example has no astrological purpose; it is used here only as an image to illustrate the thought.

7. In this connection let us note a treatise, "Sur le sens unique dans le courant du temps" by Satosi Watanabe, a disciple of Louis de Broglie, quoted by Lecomte du Noüy in *L'Homme devant la science* (Paris: Flammarion, 1946): "Our psychological life is a continuous duration: it is, as Bergson says, 'the continuous progress of the past, which gnaws at the future and swells up as it advances.' Our entire past exists integrally in our present. Our duration is not a point which replaces another point along a line, but the prolongation of the entire past, which is preserved in the present." This scholar, physicist though he be, has thoroughly "felt" esotericism, for which Time, which is "granulation," does not exist.

Only that which is invariable and undivided is real: the Present Moment, which is eternal and indivisible, cerebrally incomprehensible, but *known through our innate consciousness*. This is the esoteric world, in which high and low, front and back, right and left, cease to be, making way for *spatial vision*, which, stemming from the center, can extend in all directions at once within the volume (Space) that Spirit (Energy) forms as it coagulates into matter.

This spatial becoming is our consciousness of the continuous (esoteric), and specified genesis (the becoming of Time) is our consciousness of the discontinuous (exoteric) through the "placing" of stages or phases.

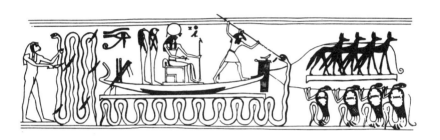

Fig. 15. At about noon, the barque of Re-Horakhty reaches the summit of a mountain where a serpent 50 cubits (26 meters) in length is found whose foremost 3 cubits are of silex. This serpent swallows in one gulp part of the stream. Seth, at the front of the boat, "directs his lance of fire against him, and causes him to cough up all that he had swallowed." (Book of the Dead, *Chapter 108). Behind the boat, a lionheaded entity runs a blade through the serpent Apophis.*

Conclusion

A RESEARCH WITHOUT illumination is the character of modern western science. This indecision colors everything, Art as well as social organization, and even, in many cases, Faith.

The West is ignorant of that serenity of which all of ancient Egypt bears the imprint.

The tombs of the leaders of this people are consecrated to their profession of faith in the survival of the soul. For these men, to die is the certitude of living again. Terrestrial life is merely a passage; the mortal body is a temporary temple for the living soul.[1]

The West labels this attitude of Wisdom a state of science that is "still mystical." But the Egyptian technique and their symbolic attest to a realistic sense and to faculties of reasoning, contradicting the view held that this epoch is "a primitive, mystical" age.

Our exoteric evolution, through the Greek metaphysical phases, leading currently to an exclusive rationalism, has given us, owing to the necessity for analysis, a "mentality of complexity" which today prevents us from seeing simply.

To cultivate oneself to be simple and to see simply is the first task of anyone wishing to approach the sacred symbolic

1. We forget, or we are not aware, that our passage through this life is a school where Consciousness must, through moral suffering, enrich its knowledge of all the higher states which Nature teaches us through its symbols. Learning is only the ABC of language which enables us to express ourselves so that communication among individuals becomes possible, but Knowledge alone is a goal that justifies our existence and the miseries of its contingencies.

of ancient Egypt.[2] This is difficult because the obvious blinds us.

One forgets, for example, that in sitting down to relax, all the fatigue goes to the thighs, the "support of the body." It is therefore worthwhile to study their role in the vital economy and the importance they have in terms of the symbolic.

One forgets that in passing one's hand over one's forehead and parts of the skull, certain tired phrenological centers are thus magnetically vitalized.

One forgets that in sleeping to restore one's energy, the *simple fact of eliminating cerebral consciousness* enables us to draw from the universal source of life, which might induce us to seek out (and find) its deeper cause.

In order to know the true secrets of life, it is necessary to abandon scientific reasoning, which is quite seductive but deceptive, and to learn how to examine that which, because we see it, we no longer observe.

Every day, at each instant, we apply "secrets" which, if we only knew how to become conscious of them, would unveil for us all the powers and all the Power that Microcosmic Man possesses.[3] There is absolutely no need to violate Nature in order to understand it, but, as the proverb says, we "do not see the forest for the trees."

In cultivating our own garden, we forget that plants grow toward the sky, that to vegetate means to rise up, and that to rise up means to make light that which is heavy, to annul gravity.

If the "group" has a new character of its own, it cannot draw it from anywhere other than from the abstract life of the individuals composing it, an abstract life that the isolated individual cannot reveal. For example, in the Unity there is a

2. This simplicity here relates to the fact of "being simple" and of "seeing simply," not to "simple ideas." Seeing simply comprises two stages (1) observing, (2) accepting—observing, without prejudice, what the symbol is, and accepting what it has to say just as it is said, adding to it neither supposition nor imagination.

3. Dr. Carrel had a premonition of this.

male nature and a female nature, which are *unknowable*. The number-entity, composed of units, reveals, first of all, this odd and even character.[4]

In Nature everything is dualized, and the *high* reveals the nature of the *low*. The crown of the tree shows the nature of its roots. The bark and the nature of the wood of this tree show—without a microscope—the nature of the type of cell which makes up this tree, because *in Life, arithmetical statistics do not apply*. Dr. Carrel has shown that each cell of the heart is

---

4. The group *manifests* the nature virtually contained in the unit.

It would nevertheless be a mistake to believe that the arithmetical statistics of the group (hence a mechanical statistic) allow that nature of a unity to be *known*, because this collectivity is itself composed of groups of simple or compound units. Otherwise, matter would have revealed the nature of the atom which composes it. Now, there is the simple atom, like that of hydrogen, and there are atoms which are very complicated in their composition, then molecules, or groups of atoms, and, further, the crystalline or amorphous states of groups of molecules. Each of these entities manifests the natural character of the components, which ultimately offers us, in matter, such a complexity of tangled "natures" that we observe this matter as being ruled by laws that apparently have nothing in common with those originally governing this world.

To illustrate this point, let us consider Numbers. The number One, presumed to be an incomposite, has, philosophically, a double nature: it is male and female (we may liken it to the Adam of the Genesis of Moses). When the first group forms the entity "Two" (which is Eve), the even number is revealed; it is feminine in relation to Unity which, *relatively,* acts as an odd, masculine number.

Insofar as this very first entity which is Three (that is, One and Two) is concerned, it manifests only two natures: (1) the sexual nature, (2) the multiplicative nature of femininity, since the number Two is the first number that can be *multiplied* by itself. We find ourselves before the first couple, the simple energetic atom called Hydrogen.

But let us now take a more complex entity, the fourth prime number which is Seven. The number Seven is odd, masculine, composed of Three (male) and Four (female). This male number Three in fact contains within itself, Eve, the number Two, manifest femininity; it is thus a complete atom and no longer a non-polarized Energy like the number One. Moreover, the female number Four is a multiplication of Two: a *square,* or a primary geometrical value and no longer only an arithmetical value.

The natures manifested by the entity Seven have nothing in common with those manifested by the entity Three. The proof is that Seven can just as well be One and Six, or Two and Five; that is, it presents in its nature that of three couples which are very different from one another. The behavior of this number in no way allows us to conclude that it is governed by the Law that rules the first couple or "primitive atom." Therefore, in order for the statistics to make possible an investigation of causes (that is, of the nature of the individual or of the unity of the group) it must be studied by means of analysis, regressively, in the various simpler groups of which it is composed.

This leads us back to Descartes and from Descartes to Microphysics, and from Microphysics we return to the "statistics" of despair, unable to understand the nature of the component without metaphysical revelation.

the heart and beats as it does. Each cell of the liver is the liver, etc.

One could cite countless examples which throw a marvelous light on existence.

But pharaonic Egypt has summarized everything in a symbolic choice of symbols it has made from the elements of its environment, a choice so wise that we must bow low before it.[5]

Every natural type is a revelation of one of the natures and abstract functions that rule the world, a verb of the divine language—that is, the entities or fully realized Principles (Neteru). They are fully realized in the sense that they are types or definite stages in the cosmic embryology of man.

Instead of starting from an imaginary construction, instead of relying on intellectual speculation, ancient Egypt shows us the path of an infallible recognition of the forces and laws that rule the Universe, by beginning from its concrete results to seek in them the causal spirit, otherwise unknowable, since all philosophic speculation is vain if it is not confirmed by facts.

Pharaonic Egypt is essentially practical. It deals with

---

5. The symbolic always applies, in every case. Every gesture, every grimace, as well as the gleam in a person's eye, reveals his impulse or secret thought. His walk, his postures, and countless details of his behavior reveal a man's character; the aesthetic tendency of an epoch, the style, architecturally, and even the nature of the preferred material, are symbols of the character of a period or a people.

Thus, one can study the symbolic of any time and any people. If I prefer ancient Egypt to India, China, Babylon, or Greece, it is because it is more accessible to us, by dint of the authentic "testimonies" it has left us, and because its entire culture is founded on a symbolic form of writing. This attests to an unsurpassable wisdom, which dared found an empire on the purely symbolic expression of its writing. Any manner of writing formed by means of a conventional alphabetical, arbitrary system can, over time, be lost and become incomprehensible. On the other hand, the use of images as signs for the expression of thought leaves the meaning of this writing, five or six thousand years old, as clear and accessible as it was the day it was carved in the stone; for a chair, a falcon, a vulture, a piece of cloth, a placenta, a leg, a human posture, etc., will not change as long as there are men on earth. This concerns hieroglyphic writing. As for grammatically constructed language, it is another question which does not come within the scope of this account.

Let us note, moreover, that Egypt's flora and fauna include many species that have never been used for the hieroglyphic symbolic. This shows a choice, hence a will to assemble the basic types of its environment that could be designated as "irreducible," for a symbolic required for a cosmic teaching (such as contained in the Osirian, and Horian lunar and solar myths).

Nature and works with natural means in which it sees the symbols of spiritual states, knowable only intuitively. The intellectual definition interests it only secondarily, as a game of thought and not as a guide. Intellectual analysis always leads, ultimately, to the necessity of choosing between the subjective and the objective; it resolves nothing, since it must consider everything within a specific duration, whereas Nature always shows us the closed, self-renewing Osirian cycle.

For instance, the principle of entropy is an exoteric supposition; the esoteric reality is a constant creation.[6]

Our mode of action requires the pre-stated theory. Ancient Egypt, which is realistic, acts naturally, knowing that theory is a fixation which limits action. Thus, one could have believed it practiced a simple, empirical science, that is, a science of application without research into causes. One forgets that there is *a rigorous method dictated by myth and symbolic philosophy.*[7]

---

6. Entropy represents the loss, in the Universe, of all Energy given off during the physico-chemical reactions of Nature. This phenomenon, considered as the final effect of this Nature (which has an equally energetic origin) places the world between a beginning and an end. This leaves to chance the sudden existence of a world in the midst of nothingness, which is necessarily understood as pure, non-polarized Energy.

Here we see, *grosso modo,* a product of exoteric, rational science, which always forces us to imprison an idea between set limits, whether in science or in sociology.

Even coarse matter is opposed, *by virtue of its inertia,* to an application prescribed by this science. Now, to go with Nature in the direction of Egyptian Knowledge is not to meet with resistance (that is, is not to provoke the opposition of inertia). We find this same teaching in Taoism, and the spiritual Judo of Japan is no other than this. Today the energetic working of the atom should show us the way.

What mechanical power must a fly develop in order to fly straight for tenth of a second, if it is really a question of mechanical power?

How do the falcon, the sparrow-hawk, and the kingfisher swoop at speeds that surpass the given facts of gravity and acceleration, and with no supporting point from which to take off?

Already our science no longer sees in *weight* a *material quantity;* rather, it sees it as Energy. Logically it is no longer absurd to admit that it may one day be possible to counteract weight with energy and even to use the energy of animal magnetism, of which it has been proved that man is an extraordinary accumulator.

7. This is why myth should be spoken of analytically. We cannot trust that we shall ever arrive at the mythical principle through the juxtaposition (syncretism) of dispersed elements, or that the Myth might be a "poetic" construction, as Professor Alexandre H. Krappe proposes in *La Genèse du mythe* (Paris: Payot, 1925). There is no *Mythenbildung* (genesis of myth) in the mythic tenet: the latter is a revelation. Certainly, if one admits that the meaning of the myth is, as Professor Krappe believes, what

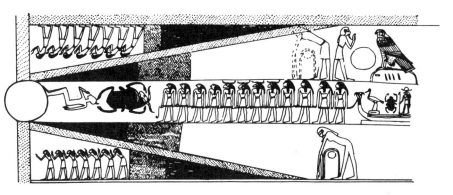

Fig. 16. The barque of the soul of Kephri-Re is drawn by 12 persons on a very singular path which enters into an immense funnel. During the crossing of the celestial waters of the Nu, followed by the crossing of the black cone, the metamorphoses are symbolized by a ram-headed scarab and a young child holding his finger to his mouth that precede the solar globe, the fruit of this "concretization" of cosmic Energy through the catalysing effect of the soul Ba and the Neter.

The directive of thought is provided by symbolic classification, that is, by the definition of the essential groups of a natural symbolic. All the functions of Nature are included in it; thing, or being (that is, the symbol-type of a lineage) represents integrally, in a vital manner, all the nuances of the functions of this part of Nature that we can in fact know. We may well marvel at the choice of these symbol-types.

he understands it to be in the light of his own science, then it is also admissible that his meaning may be purely individual imagination. But perhaps with a little modesty, one could accept the existence of a meaning that goes beyond ordinary knowledge, as Mircea Eliade suggests in *Traité d'histoire des religions* (Paris: Payot, 1926), p. 356: "Indeed, a whole series of myths, while they tell of the doings of the gods and mythic beings *in illo tempore*, at the same time reveal a structure of reality which is inaccessible to the empirico-rationalist understanding."

Explanatory legends and changes in the names of Principles may be devised, adapted to the evolution of Consciousness, but the "functional" nature of these Neteru is unchanging.

Here are some further examples of the symbolic:

The sculpted sign is hollowed out to signify entering into matter; it is in relief when leaving it is signified. This can be observed in certain tombs: the entering is that of the body into the earth; the leaving is the resurrection. What is written and figured must be read in the sense of entering or leaving. This principle applies equally everywhere, in the temples and in the dynastic style. Often, in certain scenes on a wall, this intention will be noted symbolically by the hollowing and the relief. It can be found even in the details of a single face (eyes, nose, ears). Thus, a symbol becomes a general idea. We must therefore find out what is meant by "entering into matter" and by "leaving it."

The left hand receives; the right gives and acts. In chiromancy the left hand bears the inscription of predestination; the right hand modifies destiny. This symbolism of the hands explains certain anomalies frequently observed in Egyptian figuration, such as figures that have two right hands or two left hands, or a figure joining its right hand with another's left. Similarly, since the fingers also have a symbolic meaning, one should observe the position of each of them in the gestures of making offerings.

Thus, Egypt speaks and explains through images as well as through construction.

The Principles, or *Neteru*, are either abstract (paradisiacal, created) or natural powers. The navel, by its absence or presence, shows us which.

The tableaus on the walls of the covered temple comprise up to five registers in stages. The highest row receives the inscriptions of an archetypal nature; the middle rows have those of a nature that might be called ectypal or astral (that is, related to stellar influences or astronomical cycles). The lower row bears the inscription of the formal, terrestrial, typal world. Everything must be read in this spirit, especially if one reads in it the same thing.

It must be well understood that the symbolic does not claim to be an answer to the questions which troubled humanity poses itself. The symbolic is the mean term between rational intelligence and intuitive knowledge, between the materialistic conception and the spiritual conception, which are both unsatisfactory. For this reason, the symbolic is the best tool for investigating Nature, corresponding directly to the new attitude and to the recent new means of Thought, cushioning the blow between external dualizing conceptions and intuitive vision.

It is evident that every experiment like every reasoning, necessarily must take into account, at its starting point, the "symbolic nature" of the object or of the premise, since theory, like experience, is based on the possibilities implied— or supposedly implied—in this "starting point." This is the natural (instinctive) attitude, which we would do well to render conscious by establishing the symbolic principle as a system.

On the other hand, how many medical experiments would be more fruitful if, instead of dealing with cadavers or vivisection (both always falsify the result), one dealt with the symbolic element of the living being which particularly incarnates the function under study. Each individual type in Nature is a stage in the cosmic embryology which culminates in man—an arrested stage which, as a species, shows a hypertrophied function which characterizes it.

Thus, for instance, the life, the habits, etc., of a given vulture will be much more explicitly instructive for the study of hypophysial characteristics than any research done on man, in whom the hypophysis (taken here generally) is no longer the principle glandular function as it is in the vulture, but an accessory function of the overall system. A serious anatomical study of the hypophysis in birds was made recently,[8] but these

---

8. J. Benoit, in P.P. Grasse, *Oiseaux, Traité de zoologie*, vol. 15 (Paris: Masson, 1950) p. 290, 384 ff.

observations, so far only applied to domestic birds, should perhaps have been enlarged upon and connected with the behaviors of each species, specifically as a function of the hypophysial predominance. I have yet to come across such a study of this function in the vulture, especially taking into account the influence of the intense light in the countries where it lives.[9]

Let us further note the observation of cases of accidental hermaphrodism among birds, and let us connect this with the legend of the impregnation of the "Vulture" *Mut* by the "North Wind."[10]

The definition of an attitude toward the symbol and the symbolic outlined in these few pages may be summarized by the statement that the symbol is the most perfect means for esoteric transmission.

9. Light directly affects the functions of the hypophysis.

10. Horapollo, *Hieroglyphica*, I. 11.

Epilogue

IN CONNECTION with two new basic points, "*the Present Moment*" and "*the Constant Creation,*" one can further specify that:

The creative Cause is the "scission" of a non-quantitative Unity. This scission is a "self-contemplation" which creates the Ego. It is and will always remain incomprehensible; it is the *Fiat Lux.* The Light (which later and on a lower plane will have its image in the light we see) is the direct, immediate, and final goal of this creative act. It is the Present Moment, the Constant Creation. The latter becomes phenomenal by the fact of "continuity." This continuity[1] is a series of scissions of each new unity (following the "doctrine of the elements" in the first chapter of the Genesis of Moses). If the light divides, it becomes Fire and Water. Fire in water and water in fire are a new unity, as animated Water. This, in turn, divides in "extent," that is, into above and below (heat and humidity). Once again, that which is above divides into heat and dryness, and that which is below into water and earth—that is, cold and dryness. This is procreation, the continuity of the creative act in substance and then in matter. Each procreative impulsion is ruled by the creative act, which is the Present Moment. Thus, the Present Moment *without quantity,* added to itself, forms the duration, that is, the genesis of the world (this may be compared to the *Quantum of action* in quantum physics).

1. It is this continuity, which Descartes called the "continued creation" that is not to be confused with the "continuous creation" under discussion here.

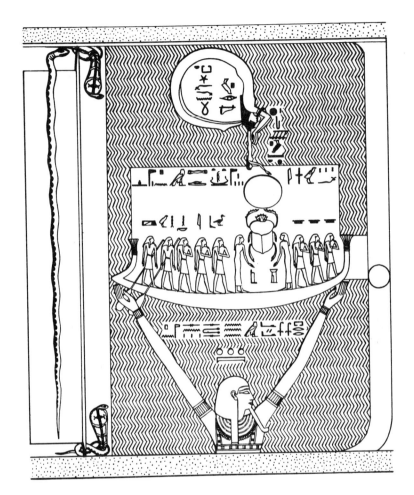

Fig. 17. Nun, the primordial waters, from which emerge the arms of Nu, symbol of the passage from One to Two and from which proceeds the Creation. The Creation is depicted by the barque of the day in which the scarab pushes the solar globe in front of him. Turning the image upsidedown, one can see Nut (the Sky) who receives the Sun. She is standing on the head of Osiris who, with his body, encircles the Dwat (the inversed world). In the barque, Hou (the Creative Verb) and Sia (knowledge) are standing next to the steering ores. (Book of Gates, *last tableau*).

Genesis is thus Time, and, as duration, it forms, through movement, Space. This is the phenomenal world.

This continuity is imperative, but, philosophically, it is not indispensable; it is procreation—that is, mediate, indirect creation—and it bears its fruit at the end of the whole duration, which is always conditioned by new scissions. This continuity is the evolution of Consciousness, which has a predestined end when all the possibilities are exhausted. Now, these possibilities are qualitatively (that is, metaphysically) implied in the Present Moment, since Creation—which always makes out of One, Two—can only engender one series of Ten, comprising Nine factors around the causal, but not phenomenal, Unity (Tetractys).

Thus, Creation is constant and has no duration in itself. It is only when the Light in turn divides that procreation or duration begins.

The following conclusions may be stated:

1. At each instant there is in the world a beginning and an end of genesis.

2. At each instant the procreative lineage may be interrupted by the creative act. This can bring an immediate end to the creature in rejecting the consequence of procreation that may be called "accident," and in reducing to its predestined essence—which, in the simple primordial act, is Light—that light immanent in the creature from the beginning. This is the Principle of Redemption.

3. Duration or procreation is not indispensable with respect to the original Cause, but is forced on the creature by "imitation"; it is the accident, and, in relation to the absolute order of *shadowless* Light which is the self-contemplation of the Cause, this duration or genesis is disorder and the division of the causal Unity into quantity.

The position taken in this study excludes the principle of a creation "making Light" within a *chaotic state*. This fact (the

Genesis of Moses) takes on an explanatory, "unreal," exoteric, character, but this *explanation*, necessary for transmitting the teaching, is thought to reveal *the reality of Creation*, which is no longer placed in Time but figures there always, without beginning or end.